Clare Phillips
was born in Rochdale, Lancashire,
and educated at Birmingham University and the
Royal College of Art in London, where she studied
Design History. She is a curator in the Department of
Metalwork, Silver and Jewellery at the Victoria & Albert
Museum, London, with particular responsibilities for
the jewelry collection. Her publications include contri-
butions to *The Illustrated History of Textiles* (1991), edited
by Madeleine Ginsburg; she has spoken on jewelry on
BBC Radio, at the Victoria & Albert Museum and
elsewhere, and is a committee member of
the Society of Jewellery Historians.

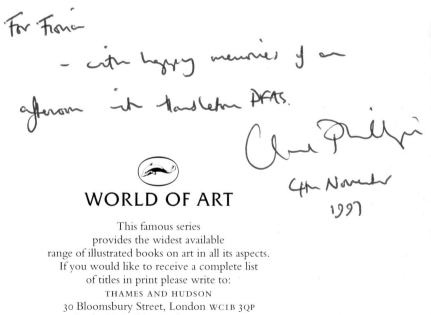

For Fiona
 – with happy memories of an
afternoon at Handletone DFAS.

Clare Phillips
4th November
1997

WORLD OF ART

This famous series
provides the widest available
range of illustrated books on art in all its aspects.
If you would like to receive a complete list
of titles in print please write to:

THAMES AND HUDSON
30 Bloomsbury Street, London WC1B 3QP
In the United States please write to:
THAMES AND HUDSON INC.
500 Fifth Avenue, New York, New York 10110

Printed in Italy

CLARE PHILLIPS

JEWELRY

From Antiquity to the Present

174 illustrations, 54 in colour

THAMES AND HUDSON

For Peter

Designed by Liz Rudderham

British Library Cataloguing-in-Publication data
A catalogue record for this book is available
from the British Library

ISBN 0-500-20287-7

Printed and bound in Italy by Conti Tipocolor

Contents

Acknowledgments

I wish to thank the many friends, scholars and jewellers whose advice and encouragement have been so generously given, especially those who have commented on various chapters: Martin Chapman, Sally Dormer, Charlotte Gere, Geoffrey Munn, Jack Ogden, Jean Schofield and Hugh Tait. At the V&A I have enjoyed the warm support of my colleagues, and particular thanks are due to Philippa Glanville and Ann Eatwell who enabled me to combine this project with my work at the Museum, and to Charles Saumarez Smith who gave the project his backing before leaving for the National Portrait Gallery; Richard Edgcumbe has been an unfailing source of wisdom and knowledge, and Marian Campbell and Antony North have generously shared their expertise; Dominic Naish has taken outstanding photographs of the many pieces illustrated from the V&A collection. Catherine Johns and Christopher Entwistle of the British Museum have advised on Roman and Byzantine sources, and Nigel Israel has kindly lent me books from his library. At Thames and Hudson Emily Lane has been a most sensitive and skilful editor, and Tessa Campbell has tracked down many elusive photographs. My family have been immensely supportive, and I owe a particular debt to my husband whose patience and encouragement have never failed and who also compiled the index, and to my parents Charles and Patricia Higgins. Finally, my thanks to Jesse Norman who has been an invaluable and incisive critic and has kept pace with the book throughout its course.

C. P.

CHAPTER ONE

The Ancient World

The wearing of jewelry has been a constant feature in mankind's existence from earliest times. Amongst scattered cultural groups the same desire for adornment is evident, each group developing its own distinctive style, and with occasional cross-fertilization resulting from trade or invasion. Our knowledge of ancient jewelry depends almost entirely on pieces that were either buried with the dead or hidden during times of war. Inevitably such sources reveal only a fraction of what would have been worn in any one period. However, enough has survived to chart the evolution of styles and techniques from the simple pieces of primitive people to those made by the sophisticated societies that began to emerge first in the Near East and Egypt.

Before people were able to shape metal or carve stone they adorned their bodies using simple beads made from seeds, berries and shells. 1 By 30,000 BC huntsmen in different regions of Europe were wearing pendants made from the bones and teeth of animals, perhaps intended as talismans for successful hunting as well as for decoration. As technical abilities developed to include the drilling and carving of stone, variety in jewelry increased. Beads remain among the most common of all artefacts found at the excavations of early settlements. This versatile form satisfied mankind's wish for self-adornment, and during the next twenty thousand years there were few further developments, beyond the ability to carve regular shapes and the addition of simple surface decoration. The next breakthrough came when people learned to work with metals.

Gold was the principal metal used for jewelry in the ancient world, prized for its rarity, beauty and malleability, and revered for its untarnishing gleam and its ability to withstand fire. It was found in Egypt, Nubia, Arabia and Anatolia, and further west in the Balkans, Spain and Ireland. The first gold was from alluvial sources, obtained by panning the gravel from river beds. As it is much heavier than other minerals, it would sink to the bottom of the pan while the debris would be swept along by the current. Alternatively, the sinking particles might be caught in a submerged sheepskin (a method which provides a possible explanation of

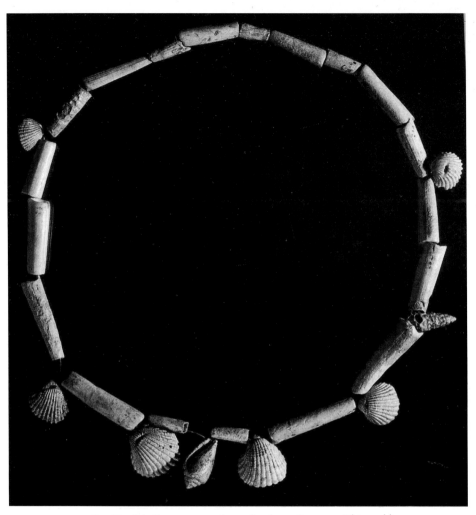

1 Fossilized shells strung together as beads, *c.* 28,000 BC. This necklace was excavated from an Upper Palaeolithic site at Pavlov in Moravia.

the legend of the Golden Fleece): the gold dust would be released when the sheepskin was dried and shaken. During the 2nd millennium BC larger quantities of gold became available, extracted from boulders of quartz by pulverizing the rock. Eventually the Romans were to develop open-cast and tunnel mining. The supply of new metal was augmented by the continual melting down and re-using of old and broken pieces. Contrary to popular belief, the gold used in early jewelry was seldom pure 24 carat, but naturally contained some silver and copper. The ratio was often as high as one quarter silver, resulting in a much paler metal known as electrum.

Most early gold jewelry was made from thin sheets, hammered out between layers of leather or papyrus. The usual thickness was around 0.1 mm (c. $\frac{1}{250}$ in.), but it was occasionally made as fine as 0.003 mm for use in funerary ornaments. It was either left flat and cut into decorative shapes, or used to cover a core of sand or sulphur for solid three-dimensional pieces. The principal decorative technique was embossing, or repoussé, where the pattern is impressed from the back using blunt punches. Bronze formers or dies were developed which enabled mechanical production of repetitive forms. Gold beads were usually embossed in this way, made as two identical halves which were then joined together. Surface details might be added in filigree, using wire which could be beaded or twisted to give a more elaborate ribbed effect; or by applying tiny spheres, a technique known as granulation.   13 Solid pieces were sometimes cast using the lost wax technique. This involved making a precise model of the proposed piece in wax, which was coated in several layers of plaster and left to set; a hole was then drilled through the plaster, it was heated, and the wax ran out or burnt away leaving an exact mould into which the molten metal could be poured.

The Sumerian civilization of southern Mesopotamia has left some of the earliest examples of gold jewelry, from c. 2500 BC, buried in the royal tombs at Ur. The extravagant funerary customs of the court meant the entombment of servants, guards and musicians along with the deceased, and large quantities of jewelry were uncovered. Made of gold, lapis lazuli, cornelian and agate, its fineness indicates that the craftsmen were working within an established and skilled tradition. Metalworking techniques were simple and effective: ribbons, discs and leaf shapes were cut from sheet gold, with a surface pattern of veining embossed on the leaves. Beads were carved in a variety of patterns in rich reds and blues, interspersed with golden beads made by covering the stone with a thin layer of gold foil. The most magnificent pieces were found in the tomb of Queen Pu-abi, who was dressed in a robe encrusted with beads   3 and fastened at the shoulder with three gold pins. She wore necklaces, a belt and a garter all made of carved stone beads, large crescent-shaped earrings, and a ring on each finger. By her side was found a complex headdress made from strings of tubular beads, gold and lapis lazuli discs and garlands of gold leaves, with a lattice of gold ribbons surmounted by a tall crest of three stylized gold flowers. Amongst her sixty-three

2 Sophia Schliemann, wife of the archaeologist Heinrich Schliemann, wearing gold jewelry dating from *c.* 2200 BC which he had discovered during his excavation of Troy.

3 *opposite* Court jewelry from the Sumerian city of Ur, *c.* 2500 BC, made principally of gold, lapis lazuli and cornelian, including Queen Pu-abi's headdress of gold flowers and other jewels from her tomb.

attendants the women wore headbands of gold leaves, earrings, chokers, necklaces, bracelets and rings, while the men wore earrings, necklaces, armlets, bracelets and pectoral ornaments.

The other major collection of jewelry from the 3rd millennium BC was discovered at the site of ancient Troy in northern Turkey by Heinrich Schliemann in 1873. Inspired by Homer's *Iliad*, he believed that he had found King Priam's treasure, hidden during the siege of Troy in 1184 BC. However the pieces were much older, made as early as 2200 BC. The most splendid of them were two intricate diadems made up of rows of fine chains which had thousands of tiny leaf-shaped pieces of gold attached along their length. These lay as a fringe across the forehead then fell as a cascade to the shoulders on each side. In addition a necklace, six bracelets, sixty earrings and over eight thousand small rings were found.

In 1922 Howard Carter and Lord Carnarvon discovered the tomb of the boy king Tutankhamun in the Valley of the Kings in Egypt. At the time of his death in around 1327 BC Egyptian jewelry was at its height, and that found in his tomb is among the most spectacular to have survived from the whole of the Dynastic Period (3100–343 BC). With its

strong colours and highly developed symbolism it was the culmination of a tradition of jewelry-making which stretched back to the Predynastic Badarian culture of *c.* 4000 BC. That early civilization had made massive girdles from multiple strings of beads of steatite (a soft stone which was given a bright green glaze), as well as ivory bangles and shell amulets.

Jewelry played a very important part at all levels of Egyptian life, adding colour to the simple white linen costumes. It was also extremely important in rituals surrounding death, and this funerary aspect is the reason why so much has been preserved. Egypt and the lands to its south were major sources of gold in the ancient world, so the royal mummies could be provided for magnificently. The dead were splendidly adorned, usually in pieces that they had worn while alive (although others of thinner gold were made specifically for funerary use), and their coffins were both covered and lined with gold. Even the poor were buried with simple necklaces. Over the centuries an immense quantity of jewelry was deposited in this way, but the greatest part of it was plundered by successive generations of grave robbers, and melted down.

The work of Egyptian jewellers was dominated by the use of distinctive amuletic devices. The repertoire of possible motifs was limited, but the designs had a magical or religious significance that was of greater consequence than mere decorative effect. The most common symbol was the scarab beetle, which referred to the sun and creation. The *udjat* eye (the eye of the sky-god Horus) was believed to offer protection from the evil eye. Lotus flowers which opened on the river Nile each morning with the sun symbolized resurrection. Other recurring motifs include figures of the various deities, reef-knots and hieroglyphs. Symbolism also underlay the use of particular colours. Egyptian jewelry was intensely colourful, drawing on a small palette of vivid materials, typically lapis lazuli, turquoise, green feldspar and cornelian (all locally available except lapis lazuli, which had to be imported from Afghanistan). According to the *Book of the Dead,* dark blue represented the night sky, green stood for new growth and resurrection, while red symbolized blood and therefore energy and life. The stones were either carved into beads or cut to a specific shape and set as polychrome inlay. In many cases artificial substitutes were used, made from coloured glass or faience – a glazed composition which can be coloured to resemble almost any stone and moulded to any shape.

6, 8

The broad collar or *wesekh* was one of the most typical Egyptian forms, made up of bands of cylindrical beads, arranged vertically by size and colour between two semi-circular or perhaps falcon-head terminals. This style of necklace appears to date back to the Fourth

4

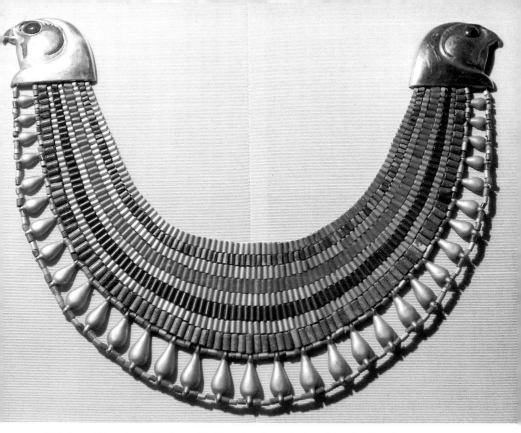

4 This broad Egyptian collar has gold falcon-head terminals and bands of beads of gold, cornelian, turquoise and faience. It dates from the end of the Twelfth Dynasty (1850–1775 BC) and was found in the tomb of a woman called Senebtisi.

Dynasty (2613–2494 BC), and remained popular throughout the entire Dynastic Period for both men and women. During the Amarna Period (1380–1350 BC), when naturalism flourished briefly, brightly-coloured faience beads moulded in the shape of leaves, petals and fruit were used. Pectoral ornaments or large pendants attached to strings of beads were the other major type of jewel worn around the neck. In most cases they consisted of combinations of symbolic motifs within rectangular frames, but in Tutankhamun's tomb (where twenty-six pectorals were found) a new style of unframed pendant was found. The motifs on the front were executed in polychrome inlay, and their outlines were repeated on the reverse in embossed gold. A smaller pendant would hang at the back of the neck to act as a counterweight. Simpler necklaces were made of coloured stone or faience beads, often shaped as cowrie shells, fish or flowers.

8

13

Bracelets were also worn throughout the Dynastic period, usually in pairs, and often with matching armlets on the upper arm. They were initially made as simple bangles, but by *c*. 2000 BC bracelets with clasps had appeared. The most typical form consisted of rows of beads arranged in blocks of different colours, separated by gold spacers and with solid panels of inlaid gold forming the clasp. They were frequently large: each of the two bracelets belonging to Princess Sit-Hathor-Yunet from *c*. 1850 BC is made from thirty-seven rows of small turquoise and cornelian beads. Tall bracelets were to remain in fashion, with hinged versions made from rigid gold panels appearing around 1540 BC.

6

Rings became more common in Egypt from *c*. 2000 BC, especially scarab rings which were used as portable seals. The scarab beetle, usually carved in stone, was engraved with a hieroglyph 'signature' on its underside, and had a hole drilled along its length. In the earliest examples it was threaded onto a linen cord which would be tied around the finger, although this was soon replaced with a stronger gold wire. From *c*. 1500 BC more substantial shanks were hammered out, with the scarabs attached by rivets which allowed them to swivel. Later still, around the time of Tutankhamun, more conventional seal rings appeared, with the name engraved on the upper face of the bezel (the decorative panel at the front). More elaborate rings consisting of sculpted figures of the gods and symbolic animals were also made, as were polychrome inlay rings with simple lotus flower motifs.

Earrings appeared comparatively late in Egypt, around 1600 BC, and at first they were worn only by women. Several hoops of gold were soldered together to form a wide, ribbed band, with only the central hoop passing through the hole in the earlobe. Other types were hollow leach-shaped earrings, or circular ear-plugs, although these were somewhat disfiguring, requiring an enlarged hole. There were also simple interrupted rings, where the lobe was eased through a gap in the circle. The same styles were made in coloured glass and faience. Two hundred years later earrings were adopted as male jewels. The pharaoh Tuthmosis IV (*c*. 1390 BC) had pierced ears, as did Tutankhamun, who wore elaborate earrings in the form of ducks.

A wide variety of diadems and head ornaments feature prominently in wall paintings and sculptures. Some, like the delicate circlet of gold wires and tiny flowers of coloured inlay buried with Princess Khnumet at Dahshur around 1895 BC, probably developed from the custom of wearing real flowers in the hair. Alternatively, young princesses might shave their heads and wear jewelled wigs, as the slightly later decorated wig of Princess Sit-Hathor-Yunet indicates. The thick hair is divided into many

5

5 Ornamented wig and crown of Princess Sit-Hathor-Yunet, *c*. 1850 BC. The locks of hair are bound with decorative gold rings. A cobra in lapis lazuli rears up at the front of the circlet (a restored replica of the original in Cairo), which is decorated with rosettes set with cornelian and blue and green faience.

locks, each of which is decorated with a large number of broad gold rings. Around the crown of the head runs a rigid gold circlet with stylized flowers at regular intervals and with the head of a cobra, the protector of kings, rearing up at the front. The choice of animal conveyed the owner's status: diadems decorated with gold gazelle heads indicated that the owner belonged to the royal harem, while only the Great Royal Wife was entitled to wear the vulture – the device of the Pharaoh himself. Men also wore diadems, and that of Tutankhamun has both a vulture's head and a cobra at the front with a curved streamer extending over his head.

Further west, on the Mediterranean island of Crete, the Minoan civilization was well established by 2500 BC. Its centre was at the eastern end of the island around Mochlos, where skilled craftsmen used imported gold to make simple diadems, pendants and daisy-headed hairpins from thin sheet metal. Little is known of jewelry of the Middle Minoan period (2000–1600 BC) which was devastated by contemporary earthquakes, but one of the finest Minoan pendants, of two bees around a honeycomb and   7

7 Middle Minoan gold pendant in the form of two bees around a circular honeycomb, 17th century BC. This outstanding piece comes from the Khrysolakkos cemetery at Mallia, Crete.

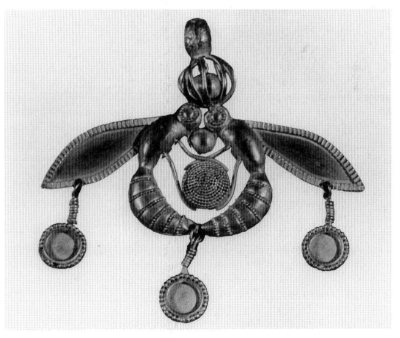

6 *opposite* Tutankhamun's bracelets, of *c.* 1336–1327 BC, arranged as they were found on his arms. They are made of gold inlaid with coloured stones and glass. Symbolic devices form the principal decoration, notably the eye of the sky-god Horus and the scarab beetle.

8 One of twenty-six pectoral ornaments or pendants found in the tomb of Tutankhamun,
c. 1336–1327 BC. These rich opaque colours are characteristic of Egyptian jewelry, achieved here
with lapis lazuli, cornelian, chalcedony, calcite, turquoise, obsidian, and coloured glass, set in gold
and silver. The motifs include the *udjat* eye, winged scarab, cobras crowned by sun-discs, and
lotus flowers and buds.

9 Greek gold jewelry from the Hellenistic period, decorated with garnets, enamel and filigree: (top) diadem of twisted gold bands with a central Heracles or reef knot, 3rd century BC; (centre) Heracles knot from a diadem, 2nd century BC; (bottom) necklace with a crescent-shaped pendant, 2nd century BC. The Heracles knot originated in ancient Egypt, the crescent in Western Asia.

golden ball, comes from a tomb of this time. Survivals from the Late Minoan period (1600–1110 BC) show the adoption of new materials such as lapis lazuli and faience, new techniques such as filigree and simple granulation, and the influence of Egyptian motifs.

By 1400 BC the Mycenaeans from mainland Greece had invaded and conquered the Minoans. The effect as far as jewelry was concerned was limited, as the two cultures had long been working in a similar style. Some of the finest Late Minoan examples were discovered in the shaft graves at Mycenae, excavated by Heinrich Schliemann in the 1870s. This period saw the development of large-scale manufacture of beads shaped as spirals, seashells, flowers and beetles. The stylized forms were stamped out of sheet gold using a basic die, then the two symmetrical halves were joined together and filled with sand. Other significant advances were made in the engraving of complex seals for rings, the use of coloured inlay and simple enamels, and the production of fine chains. By 1100 BC the Mycenaean Empire was in decline and fine crafts-manship was eclipsed for several centuries, until the Greek revival which began around 850 BC. Alongside the re-emergence of the Greeks other Mediterranean civilizations flourished, and sophisticated jewelry was made on the islands of Rhodes and Melos from the 7th century BC.

In the Archaic and Classical periods (600–330 BC) Greek craftsmen were restricted by a limited supply of gold. Some magnificent jewelry from the 6th century BC has been found in burials at Sindos in northern Greece, but most of what survives dates from the 4th century BC, discov-ered in the wealthy Greek city of Taranto in southern Italy, and in settlements in the Crimea. The necklaces are particularly beautiful, with figurative beads and pendants shaped as female heads, rosettes, acorns and melons. Earrings are boat-shaped, usually with a fringe of beads hanging below and a rosette above, or are spiralling tubes of gold which wind through the hole in the earlobe, often ending with an animal head terminal which curves back up to sit alongside the base of the ear.

In contrast the Hellenistic period, spanning from 330 to 27 BC, was rich in gold and jewelry. Under Philip II gold had been mined in Thrace, and under of his son, Alexander the Great, a huge amount of Persian gold was acquired as booty. By 322 BC Alexander's military successes had extended his empire over most of Egypt and Western Asia, and those regions contributed new gemstones, designs and techniques. One of the most distinctive features of Hellenistic jewelry is its polychromy, using specially cut panels of coloured stone or glass, and enamel. Garnets were frequently used, and even emeralds, amethysts and pearls towards the end of the period. Gem engraving reached increased levels of sophistication.

20

10 Necklace from Taranto, a Greek colony in southern Italy, 4th century BC. A fringe of hollow gold pendants shaped as buds and female heads hangs from the band of gold rosettes.

Lapidaries followed the themes and styles of contemporary sculpture, carving the stone with a bow drill or wheel, abrasive powder, and a diamond point for fine lines. Intaglios (where the design is recessed into the surface) had long functioned as seals, and were at this point usually made in cornelian or sard. Cameos (carved in relief) were a purely decorative form which originated at this time: Indian sardonyx with its parallel stripes of brown and cream was the preferred stone, as the contrasts of colour could be incorporated into the design.

Richly decorated surfaces were created by embossing and filigree. The Heracles knot or reef knot, seen first in Egyptian work, became the most widely adopted motif, placed prominently at the centre of diadems, necklaces, bracelets and rings. Crescent pendants were introduced from Western Asia, popular for amuletic as well as decorative reasons. Diadems

21

11 Late Roman jewelry from North Africa, part of a treasure of *c.* AD 400 belonging to an eminent family of Carthage in Tunisia. Polished sapphires, natural hexagonal emerald crystals and pearls make up the necklace and earrings; the ring is set with a pearl; the onyx cameo is of Minerva, and the intaglios depict Fortuna and Hercules.

12 Gold bracelets with pierced and embossed decoration, from Roman Britain – part of the Hoxne Hoard, concealed by its original owners in the early 5th century AD. The large bracelet would have been worn on the upper arm.

were one of the main forms between about 300 and 100 BC, usually decorated either with a Heracles knot at the centre or with a gable-shaped panel of embossed gold. Necklaces were typically worn from shoulder to shoulder rather than round the neck, and usually consisted of a plaited gold strap from which hangs a fringe of hollow gold bud-shaped beads. Substantial chains with animal head finials were also worn, and simple necklaces of coloured stone beads linked together on individual sections of gold wire. Gold serpents were a very popular design for bracelets and rings, their bodies spiralling around the wearer's arm or finger. Large numbers of elaborate earrings have been found, the most usual form being a disc decorated with filigree and one or more pendants suspended below from fine chains. Figures of Victory and Eros, or sirens, peacocks and doves all feature as pendants on this type of earring.

16

23

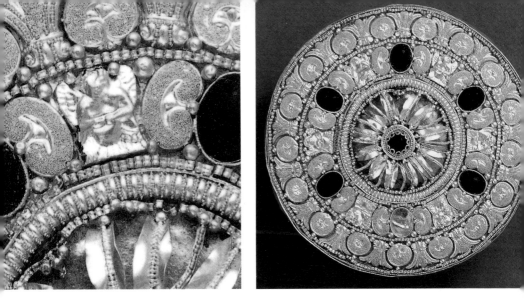

13, 14 An Etruscan ear-stud of the 6th century BC, decorated with granulation, filigree and inlay. The piece is seen here actual size (*right*) and in an enlarged detail showing the minute grains of gold applied to create surface pattern, in the technique perfected by the Etruscans.

Some of the finest jewelry from the ancient world was created by the Etruscans, who had settled in Tuscany in northern Italy by the late 8th century BC and whose civilization was at its height between 700 and 500 BC. Their reputation rests primarily on their unequalled mastery of the difficult technique of granulation, which they used to create textured surface patterning on their goldwork. Granulation does occur in the work of earlier civilizations, notably at Ur and in Egypt, but not with such delicacy and technical precision. The minute gold spheres (sometimes as small as 0.14mm/*c.* ¹/₁₈₀ in.) were probably made according to the method later written down by the 1st century AD Roman author Pliny: by heating to melting point a mixture of gold filings and powdered charcoal. The method by which they were then attached to the gold surface below without melting or being distorted remained a mystery until the 1930s. It was then discovered that a mixture of copper carbonate, water and fish glue was used to hold the granules in place, and on heating the copper fused with the gold to create a solder-less join. The process was used to create simple geometric patterns, intricate figurative scenes, and to cover whole areas with what resembles fine gold dust. Filigree and embossing were also practised by the Etruscans to great effect.

13

24

Jewelry favoured by the Etruscans includes large fibulae or clasps, necklaces either with fringes of embossed gold pendants or set with panels of cornelian and agate, broad bracelets, rings, earrings and pendants. There are two main styles of earring. The first is a large decorated gold disc or stud with a fitting on the reverse to attach it to the ear. The second resembles a box, and is known as a *baule* earring from the Italian for a travelling case. The most typical pendant, a bulla or hollow container, is usually lens-shaped and is believed to have been used to hold perfume or a charm. It was to be an influential form, and was adopted by the Romans after they defeated the Etruscans in the 3rd century BC.

14

Among the Romans the availability of gold was for centuries severely restricted, and its use in jewelry much discouraged. Even when their territories expanded to encompass gold-producing regions in North Africa, Spain and France, the metal was almost entirely consumed by the expense of military campaigns and supporting the army. It was not until the Imperial period (from 27 BC) that significant quantities were released for other purposes. Initially the Romans' jewelry followed the styles of Hellenistic Greece which had recently been conquered, but they soon found their own distinctive style, characterized by simple, heavy settings and an emphasis on coloured gemstones.

The gold used in Roman jewelry ranges between 18 and 24 carats, and it is thought that the coinage (which was officially refined) was regularly used as the craftsmen's raw material. In addition to inherited techniques, the Romans developed pierced work – often known as *opus interrasile* – where a delicate fretwork pattern is punched and cut through the metal. They introduced niello, a black composition of metal sulphides, which forms an effective contrast against gold and silver. Enamel was only rarely used, and rich colours were achieved instead with coloured stones which were polished into rounded forms. Garnets were popular, as were the cloudy emeralds from the newly discovered mines in Egypt. The latter were usually left in their natural hexagonal crystal form and drilled for threading on gold wire. In the case of necklaces, each bead would have its own short section of wire with a loop at each end, which forms the link with the adjoining stone. Sapphires, probably from Sri Lanka, were first available in the West around this time, and even Indian diamond crystals in their uncut state are on rare occasions seen in rings. Lapidaries produced fine intaglios and cameos for use in jewelry, broadly following the styles and techniques of the Hellenistic Greeks. Both amber (fossilized tree resin) and jet (fossilized wood) were highly prized for necklaces and amulets. The Roman source of amber was around the Baltic Sea,

12, 30

11

11

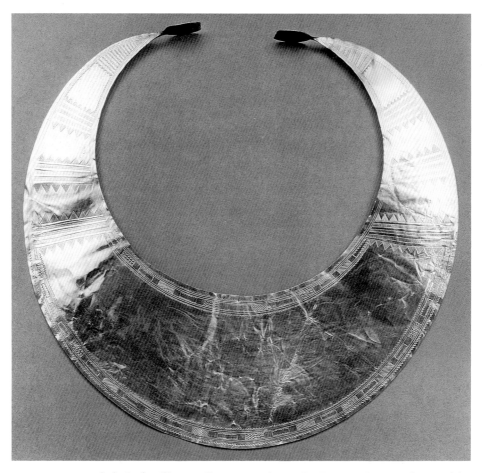

and their families to distant provinces. In Roman Britain the wealthy wore ornaments similar to those of fashionable patricians in Rome, as can be seen in the recently discovered hoard from Hoxne in Suffolk which includes twenty-nine pieces of high quality gold jewelry. The bracelets have embossed and pierced decoration (one with the Latin inscription 'Use this happily Lady Juliana'), and there are also necklace chains, rings, and a rare example of a body-chain. This harness-like ornament, known as far away as Roman Egypt and, later, in the Byzantine Empire, is a diagonal arrangement of long chains which hang from the shoulders across the body to below the waist, held in place by central roundels on chest and back. At this date the chains were usually loop-in-loop, which has the appearance of braided wire.

12

27

28

Removed from the influence of the Mediterranean world, jewelry in Central and North-West Europe developed along independent lines. Simple metalworking skills were achieved at a very early date, and burial ornaments from around 4000 BC have been discovered at the Varna cemetery in Bulgaria, made of copper and gold. Such ancient evidence is rare, but in the following centuries social hierarchies evolved which encouraged display as a way of expressing personal prestige, and this stimulated the growth of new skills and styles of self-adornment. Although there were some distinct regional styles, basic forms common to widely different localities emerged during the Bronze Age (1800–600 BC).

Ireland was particularly rich in alluvial gold, and during the Early Bronze Age the goldsmith's craft flourished. Two types of ornament were made: large discs decorated with a central cross, which were sewn onto garments; and crescent-shaped neckrings or *lunulae* (literally little moons), 17 which fastened by twisting the paddle-shaped terminals at the back. Over sixty lunulae have survived in Ireland, with further finds in Britain and France. They are decorated with geometric patterns similar to those found on contemporary Beaker pottery, concentrated at the edges and the two ends. Their form was also occasionally copied using jet beads.

In Central Europe a style of jewelry where both form and pattern 18 were created from conjoined spirals of bronze or gold wire was established during the Middle Bronze Age: fine examples have been discovered in Hungary and Germany. Bulky pieces like neck-rings and arm-rings were made in the same manner using thicker gauge metal. Alternatively in Ireland, Britain and France, cruciform strips of gold were twisted into a long three-dimensional spiral or helix which could be worn around the

17 *opposite* Many gold items from the Bronze Age have been found in Ireland; this lunula from Co. Kerry, of sheet gold engraved with geometric patterns, is typical of the early period from 1800 to 1500 BC.

18 Late Bronze Age ornaments, *c.* 1000 BC, made from spirals of gold wire found in Hungary. They comprise an element probably from a pectoral ornament (top), a pair of brooches (bottom), and two loop-pendants (left and right).

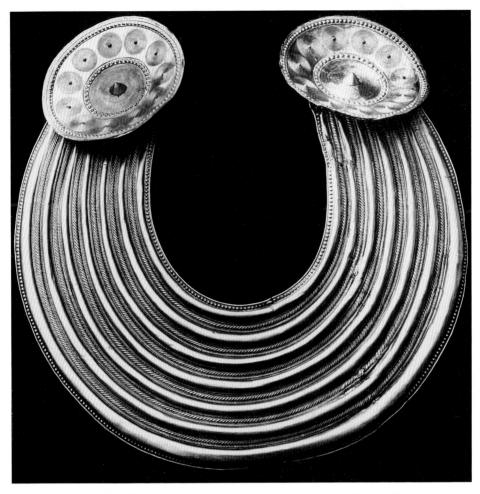

19 The Gleninsheen Gorget, *c.* 700 BC. The most splendid item of Late Bronze Age jewelry from Ireland is this crescent-shaped ribbed collar of sheet gold, with circular terminal bosses decorated with concentric designs.

neck, or coiled up and worn around the arm. Decorative dress pins, commonly of cast bronze, were gradually replaced by the fibula, one of the earliest, most widespread European brooches which functions like a safety-pin. Amber was available in some areas, and the technique for making glass beads became known in the West during this time.

During the final centuries of the Bronze Age Ireland enjoyed a major cultural revival. Typical of this later period are dress fasteners with conical

terminals; gorgets, or ribbed crescent-shaped collars with circular bosses; 19
and biconical ornaments of gold wire known as lock rings which it is
thought were worn in the hair. Large quantities of gold were still in
circulation, and one of the largest hoards, the Great Clare Find, weighed
almost 5 kg (174 oz).

During the Iron Age Europe was dominated by the Celts. Two
archaeological sites have given their names to the basic chronology
and principal styles of decoration: Hallstatt in Upper Austria represents
the simple configurations of triangles, arcs and dots of the 6th and 5th
centuries BC; and La Tène on the shore of Lake Neuchâtel in Switzerland
covers the mid 5th century BC until the Roman conquest. La Tène forms   20
are more complex and, following Celtic activity in northern Italy, influenced by Greek art. Flowing, curvilinear shapes predominate. Patterns
derived from palmettes and lotus petals are found, and the wave tendril of
Greek art appears either linking curving triangles or radiating from a
central point to form three-legged triskeles.

The most universal Celtic ornament was the brooch, which also
served as a garment fastener. Typically these are arched or bow-shaped,
with a prominent spring across one end, and a foot and catchplate at the
other which curves back towards the bow. Most are in bronze, with
cast decoration on the body and foot, and some are also decorated with
coral beads. Torcs, or neckrings, are also very characteristic. They range
from plain iron or bronze circlets to complex bands of twisted gold with
elaborately cast terminals. According to Classical writers they formed a

20 Detail of a torc or neck-ring from Erstfeld, Switzerland, from the early
La Tène period (c. 400 BC). It is made of gold, with elaborate cast decoration
which includes large-eyed animal heads juxtaposed with motifs resembling
Classical palmettes.

21 The Snettisham Torc, made from an alloy of gold, silver and copper, 1st century BC. Torcs persisted in England until the Roman conquest, and, according to the Roman writer Dio Cassius, were worn by Queen Boudicca.

prominent part of Celtic battle dress, and from excavations of burials it is clear that they were also worn by women. Later examples are found only in the regions that were still unconquered by the Romans, and by the 1st century BC they are found mostly in England, notably in East Anglia where several important hoards have been discovered. The largest, at Snettisham in Norfolk, comprises nearly one hundred and eighty gold alloy and silver torcs.

Examining the principal archaeological sites of the Western world, it is clear that most of the important techniques used in the making of jewelry were achieved by a very early date. Trade routes were sufficiently developed to allow a great diversity of materials, and to enable particular styles to spread and influence the productions of distant civilizations. While the foundations of European jewelry were firmly established, it continued to evolve, and to take one example, late Roman work provided the basis for the early Byzantine style which followed.

CHAPTER TWO

Byzantium and Early Europe

The Byzantine Empire had originated with the founding of Constantinople – on the site of the Greek city of Byzantium – in AD 330 as the capital of the Eastern half of the Roman Empire, but it survived long after the crumbling of Roman power in the West, right through the Middle Ages until 1453, when the Turks captured the imperial city. It covered an immense area: during the 6th century the Mediterranean Sea was almost encircled by Byzantine lands which also extended across Egypt and Asia Minor; and its capital remained a major artistic and ecclesiastical centre for over a thousand years. During this long period the Byzantines' fortunes fluctuated, but the empire remained essentially extremely wealthy, with a love of display and of jewelled magnificence in both the court and the Church. In 1204 Constantinople was brutally sacked and its treasures plundered by members of the Fourth Crusade on their way to the Holy Land. Sophisticated and colourful jewels, church ornaments and relics were carried back to the West, and they were to have a profound influence on the decorative arts of medieval Europe. Although the final centuries saw their territory dwindle, the artistic life of the empire remained vigorous particularly during the 13th and early 14th centuries. The few Byzantine objects that have survived can give only a partial reflection of the magnificence of court life.

The Byzantines were well supplied with the raw materials for jewelry, having domestic sources of gold in the western Balkans, Asia Minor and Greece. Furthermore, they were ideally placed for trade between East and West, and Constantinople soon became the major centre for ivory, precious stones and pearls brought from India, Persia and the Persian Gulf. The Byzantine world was hierarchical and strictly regulated, and as jewelry conveyed status, there were attempts to restrict its availability through sumptuary laws. Every man and woman had the right to wear a gold ring, but the wider use of gold and precious stones tended to be restricted to the court and the Church. The Codex of Justinian, compiled in 529, ruled that pearls, emeralds and sapphires should be reserved for the emperor's use. Financial reasons too prompted these controls: gold formed the basis of trade within the empire, and it provided the funds to maintain the army and thereby the empire's borders. Silver, for which there was a hallmarking system in Constantinople from the end of the 4th century, appears not to have been much used in jewelry. For inspiration Byzantine designers drew on their inherited Classical past, on Christianity which had been officially recognized under Constantine I, and on the oriental influences that came from their proximity to Asia.

The finest craftsmen were concentrated in the capital, and although jewellers continued to work throughout the empire, the great artistic centres of the Late Antique period such as Alexandria and Antioch dwindled in creative significance in the face of the rapid growth of Constantinople. The industry here was carefully controlled: according to the Codex of Justinian the finest materials were only available to the workshops within the palace, where a hereditary caste of skilled craftsmen produced jewelry for the emperor, his family and the court. They were also responsible for presentation pieces intended both for influential individuals within the empire and for foreign rulers. The army formed one of the largest groups of recipients, as awards were given to celebrate victories, to reinforce loyalty and to reward bravery. High-ranking civil servants also expected to receive gifts from the emperor in recognition of their service. During the 11th century the Hungarian kings were presented with two crowns made of *cloisonné* enamel panels, one of which forms the lower part of St Stephen's Crown which continued to be used for Hungarian coronations until 1916. The important role played by jewelry in the military and administrative life of the empire helps to explain the wide dispersal throughout Byzantine lands, and even beyond, of high quality pieces originating from the imperial workshops.

The splendour of the court in the mid-6th century is best seen in the Byzantine mosaics in the church of San Vitale at Ravenna. That Italian city had been re-taken from the Ostrogoths in 540 as part of the ambitious plan of Justinian I to re-unite the Eastern and Western halves of the Roman Empire. His success is celebrated in full-length mosaic portraits of himself and his wife Theodora wearing elaborate crowns, large brooches, long earrings, and ropes of pearls and precious stones, notably sapphires and emeralds. Their attendants also are richly adorned, and together they convey a magnificent vision of imperial authority.

The decorative techniques used by Byzantine jewellers during the early period were largely inherited. Repetitive motifs were embossed on soft gold sheet using a die, while chasing with hand tools was used for more individual work. Both these methods created pattern by applying gentle pressure to the surface, unlike engraving (which was used for sharper detail) where metal was actually removed using a pointed tool.

22 The mosaic portrait of the Empress Theodora at San Vitale, Ravenna, shows the magnificence of Byzantine court jewelry in the 540s. Pearls, emeralds and sapphires, which were by law restricted to imperial use, feature prominently in her diadem, collar, necklace and earrings.

When engraving was used, it was often highlighted with niello. Fine-
chiselled geometric openwork, or *opus interrasile*, remained a popular
decorative technique in the early years of the Byzantine Empire. It was
used in all types of jewelry, often to form round or hexagonal frames for
single or grouped coins mounted as pendants. Another survival was the
Roman love of coloured stones, which were to remain characteristic of
Byzantine jewelry. Precious stones were polished into smooth irregular
beads, then a hole was drilled through to enable them to be secured with
gold wire. Pearls were drilled and threaded on gold wire in the same
way. This created a very secure setting, more permanent than the
alternative straight-sided collets. The art of carving intaglios and cameos
remained alive in the Eastern Empire, and these were set in rings as well
as pendants throughout the Byzantine period.

Colour was also added to jewelry with enamels, *cloisonné* enamel
being one of the finest and most distinctive features of Byzantine
jewellers' work from the 9th to the 13th centuries. It was used to produce
detailed and brilliant pictures, often of prophets or saints, which resemble
fine line drawings filled in with a variety of opaque colours. The outline

27, 29,
30

23, 24

23 A Byzantine crown made of gold and *cloisonné* enamel plaques, given by
Constantine IX Monomachos to King Andrew I of Hungary in the 11th century
and still in its original form. It bears portraits of the Emperor (right) and of his wife,
the Empress Zoë (left).

24 The Dagmar Cross,
a Byzantine reliquary
pendant of *c.* 1000 made
of gold and *cloisonné*
enamel, found in the
grave of Queen Dagmar
of Denmark (d. 1212).
On this side are five
medallions with
Christ in the centre, the
Virgin Mary on the left,
St John the Baptist on the
right, St Basil at the top,
and St John Chrysostom
at the bottom. The
reverse is decorated
with an enamelled
Crucifixion scene.

and details of the design are in fact provided by a network of tiny
'cloisons' or partitions of gold wire soldered onto a gold backplate. The
enamel flux was made from powdered glass, coloured by means of various metal oxides. These had different melting points so could not all be
fired at the same time, and those requiring the hottest temperatures had
to be added first. Each colour might need re-filling and firing several
times to compensate for the slight shrinkage as it fused into enamel.
When all the cloisons were filled the piece would be polished to give a
smooth, level surface. A wide variety of colours could be used, but only
one in each cloison, giving a two-dimensional appearance to the finished
piece. In early examples the enamelled section stands out in relief from
its gold panel, but goldsmiths soon began to recess the area of pattern,
enabling the finished surface to be level with the surrounding gold. This
technique had great potential for figurative ornament in jewelry and was
used to decorate crowns, bracelets, earrings, medallions and ring bezels. It   23
was much favoured for ecclesiastical metalwork, panels being used to
decorate vessels or joined together to make book covers and even altar-
pieces such as the Pala d'Oro in the Basilica of St Mark's, Venice. In the
Book of Ceremonies Constantine VII Porphyrogenitos also mentions them
decorating the trappings of imperial horses.

The symbolism of Christianity pervades much Byzantine jewelry, and
pendant crosses (some of which also served as reliquaries) were among   24
the earliest and most popular pieces. In many cases the Roman forms

25 Detail of a Byzantine marriage belt made of embossed gold discs, *c.* 600. The central roundels, inscribed 'From God, concord, grace, health', depict Christ blessing the couple. The small roundels contain pagan Dionysiac figures.

persisted, with the simple addition of Christian iconography. For example, marriage rings and belts traditionally incorporated a scene depicting a man and a woman facing each other with a central figure blessing their union. By the 5th century the pagan figure of Concordia had been replaced by Christ or the cross.

From early in the Byzantine era gem-set necklaces were made from precious stones or pearls, simply threaded on jointed gold wires. Each bead would have its own short piece of wire with a loop at each end, which formed the link with the adjoining stone. Different colours alternated round the necklace, and fine examples combining prestigious emeralds, sapphires and pearls dating from the 5th to the 7th centuries have been found. Similar necklaces in amethyst and green glass perhaps represent an attempt by women of high social standing but who were not courtiers to achieve a comparable colour combination in permitted stones. These necklaces often have clasps made from a pair of openwork discs, one with a hook and the other with a ring. More complex necklaces incorporate lengths of loop-in-loop chain, gold beads and plaques of filigree or pierced openwork into which precious stones are set either on wires or enclosed in tall collets.

Pectoral ornaments in the form of large pendants attached to a rigid circlet of gold were worn by both sexes. Those of men were often collections of gold coins and military portrait medallions mounted together in a shaped gold frame, while women's versions were decorated with scenes such as the Annunciation and the Marriage at Cana. Another alternative to the necklace was the body-chain, which consisted of long chains worn diagonally across the chest and back. This was a survival from Late

38

26 Gold pectoral ornament set with coins and a portrait medallion, probably worn by a Byzantine military leader in the mid-6th century. Originally a large medallion of the Emperor Theodosius I hung below.

27 Body chains continued into the Byzantine era: this example made of gold pierced discs is of *c.* 600, from Egypt. It was worn like a harness, falling in two diagonal lines across the body with the larger roundels centred on the wearer's chest and back.

Roman times, but the chains were now made from linked openwork discs rather than loop-in-loop chain.

Bracelets appear to have been worn in matching pairs, and many different styles have been found. Bangles made up of panels of gold *opus interrasile* incorporating sentimental inscriptions have been excavated in Syria, dating from *c.* 400, and they continued in popularity for several centuries. Serpent bracelets remained in fashion from Roman times. Perhaps the most distinctively Byzantine type has a substantial hoop and a central roundel with a hinge on one side and a clasp on the other. Both the roundel and the hoop are decorated, either in plain gold with repoussé and openwork, or in more lavish cases set with stones and with pearls on gold wires. Complex and colourful decoration was also achieved using enamels, with large cuff-shaped bracelets of *cloisonné* enamel panels surviving from the 9th century.

Rings of gold, silver, copper and bronze, either inscribed or set with engraved gems, were probably made in every city of the empire. A religious inscription is a typical form of decoration, perhaps invoking God's protection or health and prosperity for the wearer. Often these take the form of sacred monograms, where the letters of a simple invocation are arranged into a cruciform device which decorates either the bezel or shoulders of the ring. Secular monograms were also much used on rings, and often spell the name of the owner.

Large earrings, favoured in Roman times, continued to be highly popular throughout the Byzantine period. The two most typical and enduring forms are long pendants and flat crescent shapes, both of which hang from an arc of gold wire which passed through a hole in the lobe of

28 Bracelet of gold decorated with pearls, sapphires and green chalcedony. Although found in Upper Egypt, it was probably made in Constantinople in the second half of the 6th century. The broad band, hinged at the back and with an opening fixed by a pin at one side of the roundel, is a typical Byzantine form.

29 A pair of crescent-shaped earrings, of gold with pierced and engraved decoration, 6th century. They incorporate the popular Byzantine motif of affronted peacocks.

the ear. The pendants are colourful cascades of mixed gemstones and pearls, suspended in clusters or on wires from a central unit which is often shaped as a double arcade. Some are of great length: 12 cm (4¾ in.) is by no means unusual. The crescent-shaped earrings are less complex, being only of gold. Thin sheet metal was used, pierced in patterns of stylized foliage, crosses or peacocks, with the finer details added using punches and engraving tools. An edging of beaded wire or hollow gold spheres was usually added around the outer curve of the crescent. The continuing fashion for ear ornaments in the highest circles of Byzantine society was in striking contrast to the prevailing custom in medieval Europe, and it was with great surprise that the Burgundian traveller Bertrandon de la Broquière in 1432 noted the Empress Maria Comnena wearing large gem-set earrings.

While Roman order and Classical traditions were to some degree maintained in the East, the history of the rest of Europe was much less settled. With the decline and fall of the Western Empire in the 4th and 5th centuries, Germanic tribes swept south taking control of a vast area. The Ostrogoths occupied the lands around the Danube and central Italy, the Franks overran western Germany and the Lowlands, the Lombards took northern Italy, the Visigoths took Spain, and the Angles and Saxons settled in England. These semi-nomadic Germanic tribes were known to the Greeks and Romans as 'barbarians', but it is clear that they achieved very high levels of craftsmanship and allowed the pre-Roman traditions

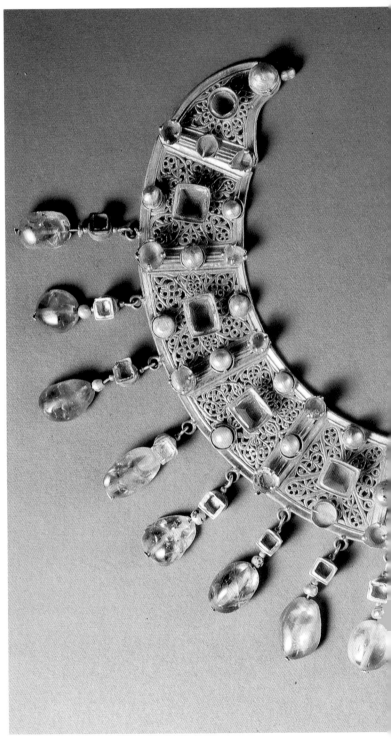

30 A magnificent necklace composed of eleven hinged plaques of gold openwork, decorated with emeralds, aquamarines and pearls. (Most of the inset stones are lost.) Probably made in Constantinople in the early 7th century, it was excavated from a site in Upper Egypt.

in these regions to revive. Although distinct groups, they were closely related, and the same types of jewelry and ornament are found throughout a wide area with slight local variations. The goldsmiths were familiar with the techniques of Late Roman workshops and the jewelry produced is of great beauty and technical complexity, combining fine materials and bold designs. Until pagan beliefs gradually gave way to Christianity it was customary to bury precious items with the dead, and this has resulted in the survival of pieces right across the social hierarchy, from kings to farmers.

Sophisticated polychrome inlay is the major feature of Germanic jewelry, worked in precious stones and coloured glass. The patterns are usually non-figurative, created by a geometric framework of cells or cloisons which in many cases covers the entire surface of the jewel, giving the effect of a stained glass window. Garnet (probably imported from India) was particularly favoured for this type of decoration. It had the advantage that it could be split smoothly along the horizontal plane, although a skilled lapidary was needed to cut the complex shapes required by some designs. Gold imported from the Byzantines was the favoured metal for barbarian jewelry until supplies dwindled in the 8th century. Then, for all items larger than rings, silver from the Arab empire was used. Less costly work was done in bronze throughout the period, and surface treatments included gilding, silver-plating and tinning. Decoration was incorporated either at the time of casting, with surface patterning in the mould, or by the separate process of adding repoussé panels, filigree or granulation. Zoomorphic decoration in the form of complex animal interlace was the most effective and widespread form of ornament.

Jewelry served a functional as well as a decorative purpose, and the most commonly found types are brooches, clasps and ornate buckles, which were used to fasten garments before buttons came into use. Brooches were made in many shapes, but most typical are simple circular disc brooches and long brooches, also called bow brooches. The latter, derived from the Bronze Age fibula or safety-pin type of brooch, were by this time more bulky and decorated: perhaps cruciform in shape, or with a semi-circular head and a flat foot joined by an arched or bow-shaped bridge. Also very distinctive are dramatic bird-shaped fibulae, which could be an imposing size: an example from the 4th-century Petrossa Treasure found in Romania is over 33 cm (13 in.) long. Paired brooches were worn by women on their shoulders to secure simple tubular dresses, and sometimes a string of beads would be hung between them. Large buckles were worn on belts, and small buckles on garters and shoes.

44

31 *right* Germanic disc brooch, made of gold, decorated with beaded wire and inlaid with garnets that were probably imported from India; found at Wittislingen in Bavaria, mid-7th century. The garnets form a pattern of interlaced double-headed serpents.

32 *below left* A pair of Germanic long brooches, of silver-gilt set with a variety of precious stones; from Untersiebenbrunn in Austria, early 5th century.

33 *below right* A pair of Visigothic eagle-shaped fibulae of gilt bronze, rock crystal and coloured stones, from 6th-century Spain. The loss of stones shows up the framework of metal *cloisons*.

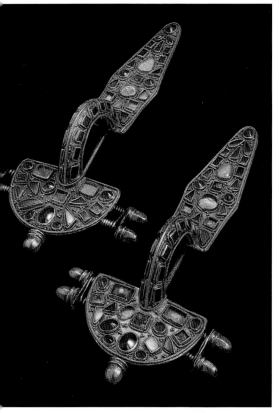

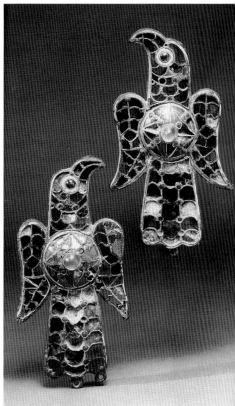

34 *opposite* A crown from the Guarrazar Treasure, found near Toledo in Spain. The pendant letters spell out RECCESVINTUS REX OFFERET – presented by King Recceswinth, a 7th-century Visigothic ruler. The combination of sapphires, emeralds and pearls set in decoratively pierced gold, and the form of the pendants, suggests the influence of Byzantine pieces like the necklace shown in Ill. 30.

35 One of the pair of gold shoulder clasps from the royal ship burial at Sutton Hoo, England, early 7th century. The red inlay is garnet, painstakingly cut to fit the intricate geometric and animal interlace design.

The first accurately documented find of Germanic jewelry was the discovery in 1653 of the tomb of Childeric I, a Frank and the founder of the Merovingian dynasty, who had died in 481. He was buried at Tournai (in present-day Belgium) in regalia of gold inlaid with garnets which included 300 bee-shaped ornaments as well as bracelets, buckles and a sword. The jewels, symbolizing of the glory of ancient France, later inspired Napoleon to choose bees as his special emblem and to have them embroidered prominently on his coronation robes. The most important hoard of Visigothic material is from a later date: the Guarrazar Treasure, found near Toledo, includes eleven crowns of gold, precious stones and pearls thought to have belonged to the 7th-century kings Swinthila and Recceswinth. The heavy gold bands have elaborate pierced decoration and pendants hanging from the lower edge. The most lavish

34

are encrusted with large collet-set sapphires, emeralds and pearls, and that of Recceswinth has a fringe of long pendants all the way round, each with a gold letter which spells his name, an emerald, a pearl and a sapphire drop. The presence of gold chains from which the crowns can be suspended suggests either a purely ceremonial use or that they once hung at a religious shrine. These sophisticated pieces indicate the great wealth of the Visigothic court, the influence of the Byzantines, and the flourishing state of trade links with the eastern Mediterranean.

The most magnificent collection of Anglo-Saxon jewelry, and perhaps the finest early 7th-century Germanic work known in Western Europe, was discovered in 1939 during the excavation of a burial at Sutton Hoo in Suffolk. The dead king, believed to be Raedwald, King of East Anglia (d. 624/25), had been given a traditional burial in a ship, which included lavish provision for his needs in the afterlife. The jewelry buried with him, made of gold and garnets, consisted of a pair of hinged shoulder clasps, a large gold belt buckle, a purse lid, and decorated fittings for a sword and sword belt. Both the ingenuity of the design and the exquisite precision of the craftsmanship in these pieces demonstrate the great virtuosity of the goldsmith.

In the Sutton Hoo shoulder clasps, the dominant elements of geometric motif and animal interlace are most successfully combined – the former in the central rectangular panels which are closely related to the carpet pages of early Anglo-Saxon illuminated manuscripts, and the latter in the surrounding zoomorphic border and the entwined boars at the curved ends. These motifs are executed in thin sections of garnet and *millefiore* glass (vari-coloured sections sliced from a striped glass rod), skilfully cut to match the stepped or curving forms of the design, and they are further enhanced by the use of a patterned foil behind the translucent garnet. The two halves of each clasp fit together at a central hinge where they are secured using a gold pin decorated with an animal-head terminal. The large gold buckle, which was cast in an intricately carved mould and then finished off by hand, is entirely covered with a complex interlace of stylized animals and birds. Their elongated bodies form an apparently hopeless tangle but can be followed from head to tail through what is in fact a very carefully controlled design.

Archaeological excavations, principally at burial sites, indicate the wealth of settled Anglo-Saxon communities and their links with the rest of Europe. The wearing of jewelry was not confined to the nobility but extended down to the level of prosperous farmers. Men might have gold decoration on their swords in addition to cloak brooches and large gold arm rings. 'Skilfully twisted' arm rings are mentioned in the 8th-century

36 Gold buckle, from Sutton Hoo, England, early 7th century. The complex interlace pattern, incorporating bird and animal heads, relates to designs in Anglo-Saxon illuminated manuscripts.

poem *Beowulf*, and they were still current in the 10th century, when according to *The Battle of Maldon* the Vikings demanded arm rings as tribute. Women of the 7th century wore rings, bracelets and necklaces of moon-shaped jewels, according to St Aldhelm. Archaeological evidence shows that lengths of glass beads (and occasionally amber) were worn across the chest, attached to the dress at the shoulders, rather than as necklaces. Earrings do not appear to have been very common. The spread of Christianity had little immediate impact on Anglo-Saxon jewelry, except for the introduction of the cross as an important symbolic design. St Cuthbert's Cross, of gold inlaid with garnet, thought to have been buried with him at his death in 687, shows that although the iconography was new the materials and techniques remained unchanged.

By the early 8th century the pagan custom of burying jewelry with the dead had been abandoned in most parts of Europe, and consequently very little has survived from the later Anglo-Saxon period, though documentary evidence such as wills and monastic inventories listing the gifts of pious citizens records many brooches, bracelets, rings, coronets and necklaces. From goldsmith's work such as the 9th-century Alfred Jewel (which was not a jewel to be worn but the handle of a precious staff or pointer) it is clear that very fine levels of craftsmanship were achieved, and that even the difficult technique of *cloisonné* enamel was known in the West. Two 9th-century rings bearing the name of King Æthelwulf of Wessex and Queen Æthelswith of Mercia (the father and sister of Alfred the Great) are of gold inlaid with niello. Niello was also used on silver for the animal and interlace disc brooches of the 9th and early 10th centuries, found from Northumbria to Cornwall. This type of ornament is known as the 'Trewhiddle' style after the place in Cornwall where a hoard of such jewelry, originally hidden from Viking raiders, was discovered.

The Vikings had never been subjected to Roman rule, and their jewelry resembles other 'barbarian' work in the dominance of animal themes and the use of repoussé and filigree to enhance a basic cast shape. They also developed an unusual decorative technique called 'chip-cutting', where the surface of the metal is worked with a chisel to create facets which glitter in the light – an important decorative element as they had almost no precious stones. The two finest pieces known are ribbed gold collars dating from the 6th century, from Färjestaden and Alleberg in Sweden. They are made of concentric gold tubes soldered together to form a broad band, and some have crouching animal figures and human faces between the ridges, worked in beaded wire filigree. From the 8th century, as supplies of Byzantine gold diminished, most Viking jewelry was made of silver which was generally woven and braided into torcs and bracelets. The island of Gotland, an important trading centre on the Baltic, produced work distinct from that of mainland Scandinavia. It is particularly known for its long brooches with square heads and for pendants known as Gotland bracteates, which are discs of sheet gold with stamped decoration and filigree detailing. Early examples were based on Late Roman coins and medals, but over the centuries the designs were transformed from Classical heads into abstract patterns.

37

The Celtic regions of Scotland and Ireland, like Scandinavia, had never been subjected to Roman domination, and craftsmen worked in a tradition that had developed independently of that of their European contemporaries. The disc brooches, long brooches and ornamented buckles which were so common in Germanic jewelry are not found at Celtic sites. Their most typical pieces in the 6th and 7th centuries are ring brooches, pins and latchet dress fasteners, all of which played a crucial role in securing garments and were worn by both men and women. The ring brooches are penannular – not complete rings – with a gap left for the pin to pass through; the ring was then swivelled round, cleverly ensuring that the brooch would not fall open and release the fabric. More straightforward are the long pins with disc-shaped heads, or those known as handpins which have terminals shaped like the stylized fingers of a clenched fist. Almost exclusive to Ireland are ornamental fasteners called latchets, which consist of a flat disc with an S-shaped hook attachment to one side.

Until the mid-7th century decoration was usually confined to the shaped terminals of the ring, the head of the pin or the disc of the latch. Pieces were cast in clay moulds, usually in either silver or a copper alloy which might be coated with tin to give the appearance of silver. Simplified zoomorphic patterns and abstract curvilinear shapes predominate, similar to those on Celtic metalwork from the Iron Age. Simple red and yellow enamels were in fairly widespread use, and *millefiori* glass was sometimes used as inlay. In the late 7th century, influenced by high quality Germanic jewelry, particularly that of the nearby Anglo-Saxons, Celtic craftsmen adopted complex interlace as their principal decorative motif and developed it to outstanding levels. Their intricate patterns of entwined curves, often terminating in stylized animal heads or feet, were not developed free-hand but with grids and compasses, and pieces of bone and slate have been found engraved with experimental or preliminary designs.

By the 8th century the shape of the Irish ring brooch had changed from an interrupted circle to a full circle with pin attached (the pen-annular form was retained only by the Picts in the north of Scotland).

37 Detail of a 6th-century gold collar from Alleberg, Sweden. The concentric tubes have long sections of ridged decoration encrusted with beaded wire; the spaces between the ridges are filled with human faces and crouching animals.

38 The Tara Brooch, one of the most splendid of the Irish annular brooches from the decades around AD 700. It is of cast silver, its panels of intricate zoomorphic decoration highlighted by gilding and gold filigree, and set with amber and coloured glass studs. The back also is richly decorated. The pin, which is twice the length shown, is comparatively plain. The reproduction here is just under life-size.

This altered the appearance of the brooch only slightly, as the widened terminal areas still featured in the design, but it does indicate a change of use, in that the ring had become a purely decorative part with the pin alone securing the fabric. These large annular brooches remained popular for the next two hundred years, worn by men on the shoulder and by women on the breast. They were made in simple copper alloy or in silver-gilt decorated with panels of gold filigree, enamel, glass and amber. Of all the surviving examples the most famous is the Tara Brooch, found in Co. Meath, which became widely known through the copies made by the Dublin jewellers Waterhouse & Co. during the 19th-century Celtic Revival.

38

CHAPTER THREE

The Middle Ages

In medieval Europe jewelry continued to be worn by both men and women, and smaller versions of adult types, with coloured glass rather than gemstones, were made for children. Although some might be purely decorative, many pieces like cloak fasteners and girdles were functional, and a large proportion had an explicit religious or heraldic significance. Medieval styles divide into three chronological phases. During the early Middle Ages, from 800 to the 13th century, the principal influence was that of the Byzantine court. Relatively little from this period has survived in comparison with the later Middle Ages. Towards the end of the 13th century the Gothic style, which already dominated European architecture, came to be reflected in jewelry. It remained fundamental to design throughout the rest of the medieval period, but from about 1375 a refining and softening of the forms and an increased emphasis on natural ornament are evident. This final phase remained current until at least the second half of the 15th century, when the influence of the Renaissance began to spread from Italy to the rest of Europe, bringing with it new styles of jewelry.

In 800 the Frankish King Charlemagne was crowned Holy Roman Emperor by the Pope, thereby becoming the first ruler in the West to bear the title of emperor since the fall of Rome in 476. In deciding the style for court ceremonial and regalia he and his successors were heavily influenced by the Byzantines, who boasted an uninterrupted Roman heritage. This influence, strengthened by alliances and royal marriages between East and West such as that of the Byzantine princess Theophano and the Emperor Otto II in 972, spread beyond the level of regalia to more general fashions. Few pieces of Carolingian and Ottonian jewelry have survived, but there is valuable documentary evidence in manuscripts. Legal codes and wills of the 9th century record items of gold and precious stones worn by the nobility: women were bequeathing chains, brooches, necklaces, earrings and bracelets in their wills, while men left jewelled sword fittings, spurs, belts and brooches. Devotional jewelry was also worn from the beginning of the Middle Ages. The 9th-century reliquary pendant known as the Talisman of Charlemagne is one   39

Few actual jewels from the Romanesque period have survived, but tomb effigies indicate that brooches, pendants, chains, necklaces, earrings, bracelets and rings were worn by the wealthy. Brooches had featured prominently among the jewels found at Mainz and remained one of the principal ornaments in the succeeding centuries. Those with pins were used as cloak fasteners, while others were simple plaques which had to be stitched on to the garment. Pendants were worn close to the neck on a riband, and a large conical ornament decorated with animals would also have been worn in this way. The sacking of Constantinople in 1204 was followed by the arrival in the West of large quantities of plundered metalwork, new ideas and a flood of precious materials. However it ultimately damaged the empire's prestige, and as Byzantine power waned, their models gradually fell from favour. Some types of jewels, notably earrings and bracelets, disappeared for several centuries, persisting only in Spain, Southern Italy and Sicily. New fashions took their place, and with the adoption of the Gothic style came a greater uniformity in European design.

The Gothic period was marked by a close connection between the forms used in architecture and those in jewelry. This influence was gradual: Gothic architecture had emerged as early as the 1140s but it was not until the late 13th century that the style was generally reflected in goldsmiths' work. It introduced pointed rather than rounded forms, and encouraged clarity of pattern and line in preference to dense surface detailing, resulting in jewels of elegant formality. Stones and pearls were now set against a plain surface or one with flat decoration such as engraving, niello or enamel. Out of this the later Gothic style developed around 1375, with the addition of naturalistic details and a general softening of outlines achieved by edging pieces with pearls mounted on prongs. Brooches, girdles, rings and head ornaments were the principal types of jewelry, later joined by elaborate gold collars which were often hung with a pendant.

Gold remained the most prestigious metal. The most valued stones were sapphires, emeralds, rubies and red spinels, which were known as balas rubies (such as the 14th-century 'Black Prince's Ruby' in the English Crown jewels). For most of the Middle Ages they were polished into irregular cabochons, which gave deep pools of colour, but in the early 14th century gem-cutting techniques established in India and Persia were mastered by European lapidaries, resulting in some angular faceted shapes. Diamonds in particular benefited from these advances, as until then they had only been available in their natural crystal form, an octahedron resembling two pyramids joined at the base. Initially the

41 Crown of the Ottonian Empress Kunigunde, from Germany, c. 1010–20, made from a series of jewelled plaques. The surface is encrusted with filigree decoration and the gems – still at this date polished into irregular cabochons rather than faceted – are set on raised arcaded panels.

42 Gold breast ornament of the late 12th or early 13th century, decorated with lions, a dog, a leopard and two griffins, and originally set with precious stones around the base. The prominent lions suggest that it was intended to be worn by a man.

oil, distilled and coloured using either ultramarine azure to give sapphire or verdigris for emerald; the mixture is then thickened over a fire, cut to the required shape, boiled in oil and put out in a hot sun to harden. Other methods required fine layering of coloured and colourless glass, or the setting of a coloured foil behind the glass or crystal. Doublets, where a thin section of real gem is glued to a false back, were also in circulation. Imitation pearls were made by mixing powdered glass, egg white and snail-slime which was then pressed into moulds, with the beads being pierced before they hardened. Sometimes imitations were used legitimately – in minor pieces, in children's jewelry, and also to decorate the funerary robes of royalty. Edward I of England, who died in 1307, was buried in robes decorated with gilt metal quatrefoils set with glass stones imitating rubies, amethysts, sapphires and diamonds. However, throughout the Middle Ages there was great concern over their fraudulent use, and various attempts were made to protect the market by legislation and stringent guild regulations.

As Europe's wealth increased sumptuary laws were enacted in an attempt to preserve the social hierarchy and restrict the wearing of jewelry to certain classes. The earliest came into force in Aragon in 1234, followed by rulings covering parts of Italy from the 1260s, and by the middle of the next century such laws were widespread. A French royal ordinance of 1283 was typical in forbidding townspeople from wearing girdles and coronals of precious metals with gemstones or pearls. A later example, brought in by Edward III of England in 1363, forbade the families of artisans and yeomen to wear any jewelry made of gold or silver. That these laws were considered necessary suggests a substantial increase in the wearing of jewelry beyond court circles, and this is further indicated by the many recorded contraventions.

44 Brooches remained the most frequently worn ornament, and ring brooches with a central pin were the most popular type. Inscriptions were the commonest form of decoration, usually a religious or amatory motto engraved in an elegant script and highlighted with enamel or niello. Alternatively the 'fede' motif of clasped hands – named from the Italian *mani in fede* (hands in faith) – was sometimes incorporated into the design, the ring being modelled as sleeves, with pairs of clasped hands emerging from decorated cuffs. Most ring brooches are circular, although quatrefoils, sexfoils, and heart-shaped versions were also made. In some English examples the gold was twisted or 'writhen' creating two contrasting bands which were enamelled in different colours. They are usually very simple jewels, but elaborate and costly examples set with precious stones and cameos have also survived.

44 Medieval gold ring brooches, mostly English or French: (top) heart-shaped brooch, 15th century; (above left and right) two brooches with the inscription SAUNZ DEPARTIR (without division – i.e., all my love is yours), also 15th century; (centre) a large brooch with gold foliage, sapphires and rubies, 13th century;

(below left) a small circular gem-set brooch, also 13th century; (below right) a brooch crowned with clasped hands, 14th century; (below centre) a sexfoil brooch of gold and enamel with a prayer to the Virgin Mary on the reverse, 13th century; (bottom) a rare double ring brooch set with a sapphire and green pastes, 13th century.

45, 46 The Schaffhausen Onyx, *c.* 1230–40, with an antique cameo of Peace in an elaborate gold and gem-set mount. From the side the complexity of the cast and repoussé setting is evident, with lions parading amongst the tall collets.

47 A large disc brooch set with rubies, sapphires, emeralds, amethysts, and pearls (now missing), of the early 14th century, found in the river Motala in Sweden. The human figures, animals and dragons are now offset by a plain gold base plate.

The 13th century produced some fine cluster brooches with ancient cameos in elaborate jewelled frames. Cameos and intaglios were very highly prized, particularly the good quality ancient and Byzantine examples which were removed from earlier settings and re-used. The most splendid example of this type to survive is the Schaffhausen Onyx, with a central cameo of Peace in a gold frame set with sapphires, turquoises, pearls, emeralds, rubies and garnets, amidst which are tiny gold lions and eagles, symbolizing strength and nobility. It has no pin on

45, 46

50 *Email en ronde bosse*,
a technique which first
appeared in the 1360s,
is used to enamel the three-
dimensional figures in this
brooch of two lovers in
a garden enclosed by a
woven wattle fence; it is
also set with a diamond,
a ruby and pearls. German
or Burgundian,
c. 1430–40.

and with pearls mounted on prongs around the edge. Many were made
in Paris, and they were particularly popular at the Burgundian court. A
series of sixteen, thought to have been made in Cologne in the early 15th
century, have been preserved in the treasury of Essen Cathedral. Jewels
sometimes incorporated initial letters, which might have a personal
association or devotional significance. A brooch from *c.* 1400 in New
College, Oxford, consists of an Annunciation scene framed within a
Gothic letter M for the Virgin Mary. Also typical of late Gothic naturalism is the 'dry branch' motif where the gold is patterned to resemble
50 bark. This was used to create the wattle fence in a 15th-century brooch
showing a pair of lovers in a garden.
51   Girdles, or long belts, were an essential part of dress for both men and
women right through the Middle Ages, although little is known of their
design before about 1150. Most are in plain leather, but they could be
very richly decorated, with elaborate buckles and belt-ends, and studded
along their considerable length with mounts made of silver, silver-gilt
and enamel. Such ornate girdles usually had a specially woven silk or

66

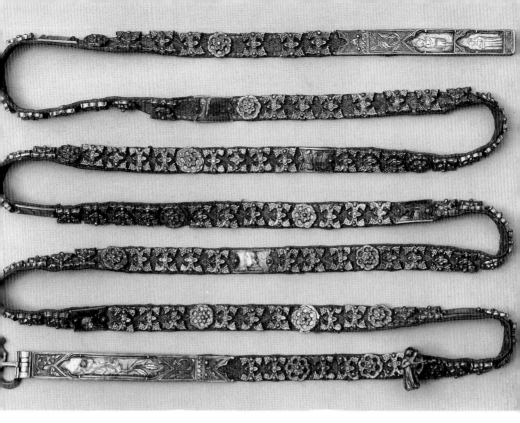

51 This girdle, with silver-gilt mounts and *basse-taille* enamelled ends on a wool base, is from Venice, *c.* 1350–70. It is some 177 cm (over 68 in.) long. The engraved figures, and the half-human grotesque forming the buckle, are similar to decorations in contemporary illuminated manuscripts.

52 In his effigy in Cracow Cathedral, *c.* 1370, King Casimir III of Poland wears a sword-belt decorated with architectural elements. His crown shows the tall fleurons typical of the late 14th century.

velvet base rather than leather; the metal mounts would have been purchased separately, and might be detached and re-used many times. In the Gothic period these mounts are typically architectural motifs, decorative initial letters or heraldic devices. Women's girdles tend to be wider than men's, except during the 14th-century fashion for men to wear wide girdles made of oblong metal plaques around their hips. A prime example of the latter is the architectural girdle or sword belt from *c.* 1370 on the effigy of King Casimir III of Poland in Cracow Cathedral. With the growth of devotional jewelry in the 15th century girdles were embroidered with religious quotations and figures of the saints. More frivolous pieces were also made, such as one that Philip the Good, Duke of Burgundy, wore for dancing in 1420, which had bells attached. Girdles were also used for hanging purses, keys, paternosters (the forerunners of the modern rosary) and pomanders from the wearer's waist. These items, like the decorated belt-ends, were always vulnerable to theft by cut-purses.

Rings were worn on all fingers, and on more than one joint. Many were simple gold bands, perhaps with a sentimental or religious inscription decoratively engraved. The gems are held in place either by claws or by the extension of the surrounding gold over the widest part of the

52

53

53 Medieval rings: Back row, left to right: (1) gold signet, English, 15th century; (2) gold devotional ring with three engraved bezels depicting St Edmund, St John the Baptist and the Virgin and Child, English, late 14th century; (3) gold signet, set with a sard intaglio of a male bust, engraved around the bezel IOHANNES:EST: NOMEN:EIUS (John is his name), probably English, late 13th century; (4) gold signet, *c.* 1300, engraved around the bezel TECTA:LEGE:LECTA:TEGE (read what is held, hold what is read), the sapphire intaglio of a veiled lady probably carved in Paris; (5) gold, set with a sapphire and four small amethysts, 13th century; (6) gold, set with a drilled sapphire (see p. 59), English, *c.* 1360; (7) silver signet ring engraved with a pair of shears, English, *c.* 1500. Front row, left to right: (1) gold stirrup ring set with a sapphire, 13th century; (2) gold posy ring, inscribed EL:WERE:HIM:YAT:WISTE: TO:WHOM:HE:MIGTE:TRISTE (he is fortunate who knows whom he can trust), English, *c.* 1300; (3) gold, set with a sapphire, early 14th century.

54 The Crown of Princess Blanche, *c.* 1370–80. It is of gold, set with sapphires, rubies, pearls and diamonds and eight 14th-century imitation diamonds, and with enamelled decoration around the circlet. In the late 14th century crowns became taller with elongated fleurons, which here alternate with smaller fleurons.

stone to enclose it in a solid frame. In both cases the bezel is usually an irregular shape because cabochon stones are seldom symmetrical. Bezels became increasingly elaborate, moving from the simple stirrup-shaped rings of the late 12th century to tall Gothic compositions with decorated shoulders. Engraved gems were set as signet rings, used for sealing letters and documents, although versions made entirely of metal were cheaper and more common. Rings were engraved with religious images and figures of the saints, particularly in 15th-century England, and the band of

55 Medieval devotional jewels: (left) a French reliquary pendant portraying St Catherine of Alexandria, of silver-gilt and *basse-taille* enamel, *c.* 1370–90; (centre below) a French reliquary pendant made from an Islamic rock crystal flask shaped as a fish, with silver-gilt mounts, *c.* 1300; (centre above, and right) two German pendants depicting the Nativity and the Crucifixion, both of silver-gilt, late 15th century. The Nativity scene was achieved by casting the figures in relief and applying them to the disc; the Crucifixion pendant was cast in one piece and then gilded.

humble materials were considered more suitable by the wealthy and poor alike. Early examples reproduced the seal of the particular church, but in time more representational images appeared, specific and easily recognizable as being connected with a particular saint or shrine. A saint's cult could spread rapidly: in England, St Thomas Becket was martyred at Canterbury in 1170 and by 1179 pilgrim badges were being sold at his shrine. Reliquary pendants are also a characteristic type of medieval 55 jewel. Rock crystal, a material both precious and transparent, was ideal for this purpose, and the perfume flasks carved by Fatimid craftsmen in Egypt several centuries earlier were particularly prized. Remounted in the West, they were usually worn at the waist suspended from a chain.

Another type of religious jewel was the Agnus Dei medallion, made of wax and bearing an image of the Lamb of God and the name of the current pope. From at least the 1130s they were made at St Peter's in Rome on the Saturday before Easter each year: some were distributed by the pope at mass that day, while others were dispatched as papal gifts to kings and emperors. Wax itself was an expensive commodity in the Middle Ages, but it was for their spiritual and prophylactic qualities that 'Agnuses' were so highly prized. These included the power to efface sins, increase piety, protect from fire, shipwrecks, storms and the attacks of the devil, and to help women during labour. For wearing they were mounted in a frame and hung from a girdle or round the neck. Very few have survived despite the number that must have been in circulation at the time. Such was their appeal that the trade in imitations flourished, particularly during the 15th century.

From the late 13th century onwards the most extravagant devotional jewels were paternosters, sets of beads strung according to a cycle of 56 prayers. The beads, often to be seen in portraits hanging from a girdle or around the wrist, were usually threaded in groups of ten called decades, either as a continuous loop or as a string with an elaborate finial or tassel at the end. Although they could be modest items, even made from a length of knotted cord, there was a great demand for paternosters in the finest materials. These included coral from around Sicily and Naples, amber from the Baltic, jet from Whitby and Santiago de Compostela, German agates, rock crystal, Venetian glass and gold. Many had pendants of silver-gilt – a crucifix, the figure of a saint or an initial letter. They were manufactured all over Europe, and in 14th-century London there were sufficient craftsmen making them to give rise to the naming of two 'Paternoster Lanes'. Although in essence they were religious pieces, they became such splendid symbols of status that their wearing was at times restricted: in the late 13th century members of the Dominican

56 Contemporary jewelled pendants and a paternoster (hanging at the right) were used by the miniaturist to frame this scene of the Annunciation in a Flemish Book of Hours, *c.* 1500.

and the Augustinian religious orders were forbidden to wear beads of coral, amber or crystal. By the end of the 15th century a reforming preacher in France was even giving sermons where paternosters were cited along with worldly wealth and mistresses as things to be renounced by the pious.

The Renaissance to 1630

The transition from the Gothic style to that of the Renaissance, reflecting a new interest in the culture and arts of ancient Greece and Rome, occurred gradually in Europe. In jewelry there was no direct influence from Classical pieces, which were as yet unknown, but decorative motifs from Classical architecture became widespread and mythological subjects became a popular alternative to biblical scenes for figurative pieces. This new type of jewelry design first appeared in Italy during the second half of the 15th century, but in Northern Europe the Gothic style persisted until the early 16th century. The Renaissance was a time of extraordinary splendour, and with new sources of gemstones, more jewelry was worn than ever before. Surviving pieces, most commonly rings and pendants, show the high levels of craftsmanship and the intricacy of design that were achieved during this period, but it is through contemporary portraits that the full magnificence of court jewelry can be best appreciated. They illustrate the lavish quantities worn by both men and women, and the precise, naturalistic style of painting during this period means that it is depicted in minute detail.

In the late 15th century the major Italian city states were extremely wealthy and their princely families were great patrons of the arts. This created a favourable atmosphere for goldsmiths' work and for the proliferation of new fashions in jewelry. One of the most striking changes evident in portraits by the 1470s is the abandoning of bulky medieval headdresses. Instead the hair was carefully arranged and dressed with strings of pearls and jewels, such as the narrow cord encircling the crown of the head which was later known as a *'ferronnière'* after Leonardo da Vinci's painting, *La Belle Ferronnière*. The new styles were introduced to the rest of Europe by royal gifts and dowries, and by itinerant gold-smiths whose numbers were increased by wars and religious persecutions. The circulation of engraved designs, which for the first time could be printed in large quantities, ensured the rapid international spread of new fashions.

In general men were more richly jewelled during the first half of the 16th century and women during the second. In England, following the

57 King Henry VIII of England encouraged the wearing of lavish jewelry for men. In this portrait after Holbein, of *c.* 1536, he wears jewelled ornaments on his slashed doublet and sleeves and on his hat, an elaborate gold chain with alternate H-shaped links, and a gem-set pendant, as well as several rings.

58 New fashions spread from Italy, where by the 1470s bulky head-dresses had been abandoned in favour of the *ferronnière* (a narrow cord encircling the head) and jewels attached directly to the hair. Both are seen in this portrait of the Florentine noblewoman Barbara Pallavicino by Alessandro Arnaldi.

57 Act of Supremacy in 1534, Henry VIII used the confiscated riches of church treasuries to fund his lavish patronage of the arts which included the commissioning of splendid pieces of jewelry. In portraits he is shown wearing heavy collars and rings, his doublet and sleeves studded with gem-set clasps, and with a row of jewels on his hat. The fashion for cloth-ing with regular slashes cut in the fabric, to allow the shirt beneath to be pulled through, was complemented by the use of jewelled clasps to hold 64, 67 the strips of cloth together. Contemporary French fashions were led by Francis I, whose portraits show a similar love of display, with a preference for thinner bar-shaped ornaments known as aglets (from the French *aiguillette*, little needle) attached to the ribbons fastening his slashed 73 costume. During the second half of the century the influential court of Philip II of Spain promoted a more restrained style with very little jewelry for men, while in England Elizabeth I's long reign ensured that pieces worn by women increased in extravagance.

76

In Germany the strong Gothic tradition was first challenged in 1494 with the Renaissance jewelry brought from Milan by Bianca Maria Sforza on her marriage to the Emperor Maximilian I. The response was slow, however, partly because the Renaissance style in other areas of art had not yet reached Germany, and partly because of the discouraging effect of the Reformation. When the new style was adopted it spread rapidly, and by the mid-16th century the wealthy cities of Munich, Nuremberg and Augsburg were attracting goldsmiths and designers from all over Europe, and had become major centres for jewelry production. Designs of the 1540s such as those by the Nuremberg painter and engraver Virgil Solis (1514–62) show the skilled use of Renaissance ornament in the enamelled strapwork and shaped collets of complex chains, necklaces and pendants. The magnificent pieces of this type worn by Duke 59 Albrecht V of Bavaria and his consort Anna in mid-16th-century Munich were recorded in a detailed inventory painted by the artist Hans Mielich.

The voyages of discovery sponsored by the Spanish and Portuguese courts at the end of the 15th century significantly affected the gem trade. Columbus's discovery of the New World in 1492 greatly augmented the meagre supplies of emeralds available in Europe, and together with large quantities of South American gold and silver, these gemstones brought Spain immense wealth. At first precious materials were plundered from temples and burial sites, but by the mid-16th century the Spanish had discovered the source of the emeralds in Colombia and established mines. Barcelona became their trading centre for gems, and developed

59 A necklace of c.1550–60, painted by Hans Mielich as part of the illustrated inventory of jewelry belonging to Duchess Anna of Bavaria. The rich piece, set with gems and pearls, is displayed within an elaborate Mannerist frame.

a flourishing goldsmiths' guild whose records include an important series of apprentices' designs known as the *Llibres de Passanties*. The Portuguese navigator Vasco da Gama discovered the sea passage to India by sailing around the Cape of Good Hope in 1498. India was to be the main supplier of diamonds throughout the Renaissance, and this new route soon superseded the slower overland routes that merchants had used for centuries. Lisbon gradually replaced Venice as the principal city through which Indian gemstones arrived in Europe, and the Portuguese were brought into the forefront of the gem trade.

For most of the 16th century the principal European centres for cutting and polishing diamonds were Antwerp (which replaced Bruges where the harbour had silted up) and Paris. With the Sack of Antwerp in 1585 many craftsmen fled to Amsterdam and established diamond-cutting there. Table-cut stones were the most common. They were sunk into closed-back settings and their dark glitter – in paintings table-cut diamonds appear black – is a very distinctive feature of the jewelry from this period. In the early 17th century European lapidaries devised the rose cut, which enabled the gems to sparkle more brightly. This has a flat base and a domed top covered with small triangular facets. The earliest known design showing rose-cut diamonds is from 1623, by the Frenchman Petrus Marchant, who used them in combination with square table-cut diamonds. Rubies were highly prized during the Renaissance, particularly the deep red variety from Burma. Emeralds and sapphires were also much used, and pearls remained one of the most costly and desirable gems. The art of cameo carving was reintroduced in various European cities, notably Milan, adding to the Classical cameos and engraved gems already collected by many Renaissance princes. Both ancient and contemporary examples were set in enamelled gold frames to make rings, pendants and hat jewels.

The production of imitation gems and pearls flourished with increased sophistication. In 1502 the false pearls made in Venice were felt to be such a threat to the city's reputation for real pearls that making them was punishable by loss of the right hand and a ten-year exile. As in the medieval period, coloured stones were achieved with glass, foils, and slivers of genuine gemstone made into doublets. Imitation diamonds were cut from rock crystal or glass, and with the Portuguese occupation of Sri Lanka a further alternative, colourless zircon, became available.

The concept of 'Crown jewels', as distinct from the personal jewelry of a royal family, originated in the Renaissance, when in 1530 Francis I declared eight particularly fine pieces to be inalienable heirlooms of the French kings. This was followed by similar rulings by other monarchs which laid the foundations for the great royal treasuries of Europe. The protection referred only to the stones and not to their settings, allowing Crown jewels to be re-worked from one generation to the next. Pieces unprotected by such laws were regarded as portable wealth, and they played a crucial role in the major financial transactions of Europe. Merchant banks such as the Augsburg house of Fugger combined their position at the centre of the international money market with dealing in the finest gemstones and pearls. Bank loans often consisted partly of jewelry, as happened when Henry VIII arranged a loan from Antwerp bankers in 1546. Particularly important jewels were given names, and the movement of these identifiable pieces within Europe often mirrored the fortunes of their princely owners. The 'Three Brothers' pendant of three large rubies was first owned by Charles the Bold, Duke of Burgundy, from whom it was captured by the Swiss in 1476. It was acquired by the Fuggers who sold it to Henry VIII, and it is depicted in portraits of Elizabeth I and James I before the rubies were reset for the future Charles I in 1623. It is last mentioned in Amsterdam, pawned during the English Civil War to raise money for the Royalist cause.

73

The names of many Renaissance jewellers are known, although attributing particular pieces to them is seldom possible. The most famous is the Italian Benvenuto Cellini (1500–1571), who worked in Rome and for the French king Francis I at Fontainebleau. His autobiography and treatises give a vivid insight into the period and indicate that he was a prolific craftsman. No known examples of his jewelry have survived, although the large gold morse, or clasp, that he made for Pope Clement in 1530–31 was recorded in watercolours before it was melted down at the end of the 18th century. Throughout the 16th century the gold-smith's craft was regarded as one of the most prestigious, and was closely linked to the arts of sculpture and painting. In Italy it was common for fine artists to train also as goldsmiths, with Botticelli and Donatello amongst the many who did. Conversely, goldsmiths such as Cellini and his rival Cristoforo Foppa, known as Caradosso (c. 1452–1526/27), were also skilled in sculpture and painting. This alliance created a new approach to jewelry which applied in miniature the standards of precision and clarity required in sculpture. It also contributed to the beautiful and realistic depiction of jewelry in paintings. In Northern Europe this combination of artist and goldsmith was rarer. However the Nuremberg painter Albrecht Dürer (1471–1528), whose father was a goldsmith, designed some jewelry; and Hans Holbein (1497?–1543), originally from Augsburg but working in London at the court of Henry VIII, made over two hundred designs for chains, hat badges and pendants.

60

60 Design for a monogram pendant based on the letters RE, by Hans Holbein, court painter to Henry VIII, *c.* 1532–43. Jewels of this type often combined the initials of a husband and wife.

61 *opposite* Mid-16th-century devotional pendants: (left to right) the Pelican in her Piety, of enamelled gold set with a ruby, from Spain; the sacred monogram IHS, of hog-back diamonds set in gold, from northern Europe; and the Tor Abbey Jewel, an English *memento mori* pendant where the enamelled gold skeleton is intended as a reminder of man's mortality. The coffin is decorated in enamel with a moresque pattern, and inscribed around the edge THROUGH:THE:RESURRECTION:OF:CHRISTE: WE:BE:ALL:SANCTIFIED.

During the first half of the century parures or sets of matching jewelry were very important for both men and women, and Henry VIII had at least two which included pieces such as a broad collar, a pendant and chain, dress clasps and hat jewels. Jewelry worn by early Tudor ladies tended to be less ostentatious, and consisted of matching panels of pearls and precious stones arranged in narrow bands which had different names according to where they were worn. Those attached to a head-dress were called 'biliments', while those stitched around a wide square neckline were called 'squares'. The set usually included a necklace called a 'carcanet' and a long girdle. Non-suited ornaments such as pendants were worn at the neck, and further variety could be achieved by hanging a jewelled pomander or miniature book from the girdle. By the mid-16th century low square necklines had been replaced with high collars opening at the front to reveal the beginnings of a ruff. Necklaces became longer, and women's dress jewels were arranged all over the bodice and sleeves rather than as borders around their edges.

Pendants were one of the favourite types of Renaissance jewel, and pieces of great imagination and novelty were made. They were usually worn on long gold chains, but could also be attached to a lady's bodice

57

67

61–63

or sleeve. They were made to be seen from either side and so were always decorated on the back, often with an enamelled pattern of scrolling lines and pointed leaves known as moresque decoration. Although some pendants were obviously made to match a necklace or elaborate chain, they were usually individual jewels, and added variety and perhaps humour to the more formal parures. They range from single gemstones set in elaborate enamelled gold surrounds to miniature figures sculpted in gold and decorated with enamels and precious stones. Some had a clear functional role, such as the toothpicks and earpicks that were worn from the late 15th century onwards. The medieval faith in the magical and medical qualities of particular materials had diminished but not disappeared completely, and narwhal ('unicorn') horn was still prized as a detector of poisons. Devotional jewels remained popular throughout Europe, ranging from simple crucifixes to complex symbolic pieces. As with secular jewels, many took the form of miniature sculptures suspended on short chains. These might show the Virgin and Child, or a symbol of Christ such as the Lamb of God or the Pelican in her Piety, 61 where the pelican draws blood from her own breast to feed her young. At the same time pieces of great frivolity were made, drawing on

81

62 A late 16th-century Spanish pendant of a woman with a feather headdress riding on a hippocamp (a mythical sea creature, half horse and half fish). The piece is of gold, decorated with enamel and pearls and set with cabochon emeralds probably brought from the New World.

Classical mythology and real or imaginary beasts and birds. As befitted an era of maritime exploration miniature ships, sea-monsters, mermaids and mermen were also popular.

62, 67

Pendants were designed around initial letters and monograms, sometimes combining the first letters of the names of a husband and wife. These highly personal jewels seldom survived long after the lifetime of their original owners, as the details were so specific. The devotional equivalent used the initials of the sacred monogram IHS, derived from the Greek word for Jesus (also interpreted as the contraction of the Latin 'Jesus Saviour of Men'). The angular outline of the initials was particularly well suited to rectangular hog-back diamonds, set edge to edge to form the letters surmounted by a cross. The backs of these jewels were richly enamelled, usually with symbols of Christ's Passion.

The engraver Erasmus Hornick, from Liège, published a series of designs for arched or tabernacle-shaped jewels during the 1560s which were to have a great influence on pendant design during the later 16th century. They consist of a gold architectural frame around a central niche containing a figurative scene such as the Adoration of the Magi, or a personification of Faith, Hope or Charity. Conveniently for the goldsmith, the basic shape could be cast in large quantities, yet a wide variety of themes was possible and the customer was able to choose the central figures, which were applied separately. In the 1590s a more delicate version of this basic form was developed by Daniel Mignot, a Frenchman working in Augsburg. He published engravings for pendants made from several layers of openwork panels which were fastened together with tiny screws. These were lighter and therefore more economical.

63 Engraving of a design by
Daniel Mignot for a tabernacle pendant
depicting Hope, surrounded by patterns
for enamelled decoration, 1593.
Developments in printing allowed designs
to be reproduced in large quantities,
and fashions became more consistent
across Europe.

64 *above* This man painted by the
German artist Hans Mielich in 1548
wears a circular gold badge and scattered
aglets in his hat. He also has a pendant
whistle on a long gold chain, and pairs
of rings on three fingers.

65 *above right* A dress ornament, of
pearls and precious stones set in colourful
enamelled gold; German, *c.* 1600.

66 *right* Dress ornaments set with table-
cut stones decorate the shoulders and
oversleeves of the gown of Magdalena of
Bavaria, Duchess of Neuberg, painted by
Peter Candido in 1613. Her necklace,
with its human figures in enamelled gold,
shows the Renaissance love of elaborately
sculpted settings.

67 *opposite* Lady Cobham, portrayed in
1567, has gold aglets on her gown; her
headdress has a row of jewels – or biliment
– attached, and she wears a heavy gold
necklace with a ship pendant. Her
daughters wear identical pendants
and chains.

Court dress was very richly jewelled in the 16th century, and dress ornaments were made in large quantities to decorate the gowns, doublets and hats of both women and men. When the fashion for slashed costume waned, clasps and aglets became purely ornamental – small enamelled gold trinkets or clusters of stones attached at regular intervals all over the bodice and sleeves of a dress. There was immense variety and charm possible in these small jewels; Elizabeth I is recorded as having been given ones shaped as stars, tortoises and faces. Aglets, worn in pairs, remained popular despite their more overtly functional form, and can be seen scattered over Lady Cobham's gown in the family portrait of 1567. Comparatively few dress jewels have survived. Some of the finest, which were amongst the jewelry belonging to two Habsburg archduchesses who entered a convent near Innsbruck in Austria in 1607, were preserved as decorations on a chalice and the crown on a statue of the Madonna.

Soft velvet caps were worn by men both indoors and outdoors, and throughout the Renaissance they were generally decorated with badges which ranged from simple gold buttons and aglets to complex jewels. Henry VIII is often portrayed wearing a row of jewels alongside the ostrich feather in his cap, matching those on his doublet and sleeves. However, the most typical hat jewel is a circular medallion in gold, decorated with a scene from either the Bible or Classical mythology. Cellini describes the popularity of these hat badges in Italy during the 1520s, and remarks how expensive they were because they were so laborious to make. He tells us that both he and Caradosso produced a large number. Most scenes required several figures which were worked in high relief, and some were enamelled and set with precious stones as well.

With the development of European cameo carving, hat jewels with cameo portraits set in enamelled gold frames became popular. Alternatively, carved hardstone and enamelled gold were more closely combined in the complex *commessi* jewels, where the picture was created by integrating the two materials. In the *commesso* hat jewel depicting Leda and the swan from the imperial collection in Vienna, the head and torso of Leda are carved from one piece of white chalcedony and her foot from another, with folds of textured gold 'cloth' arranged in between. The swan and the attendant Cupid are of enamelled gold, as is the rich architectural background. Around the medallion is a frame of fleurs-de-lis decorated with enamel and table-cut stones. It is not known where these *commessi* jewels originated but they were particularly prized at the French court.

During the Renaissance rings were more richly ornamented than ever before, with gemstones or cameos set in intricately sculpted and

68 Hat jewel depicting Leda and the Swan with Cupid in attendance, French,
c. 1550–60. The figure of Leda is carved from white chalcedony, which is skilfully
integrated into the surrounding enamelled gold to create what is known as a
commesso. The eight fleurs-de-lis in the jewelled and enamelled frame suggest that
it might have been a royal commission.

chased gold to which coloured enamel decoration was added. As in the
preceding centuries, rings were worn in profusion on both fingers and   57, 64
thumbs, and on different joints of each finger. An inventory of Henry
VIII's jewels drawn up in 1530 lists 234 rings, and accounts of visitors to
the court show that it was customary for him to wear many at the
same time. The scientific interests of the Renaissance resulted in rings
which had compasses or sundials contained in their bezels. With the
development of watch-making in the 16th century, rings containing   69
miniature timepieces were also made, particularly in Augsburg. By the
early 17th century these could even strike the hour, although this made

69 Watch ring, with the mechanism (including an alarm) contained in the bezel, made in Augsburg, c.1580. A miniature enamelled altarpiece, with the Crucifixion flanked by wings displaying the instruments of the Passion, unfolds from inside the lid. The ornate sculpted shoulders include caryatid figures.

the rings both heavy and costly. Rings might have a secret compartment inside the bezel underneath the gem-set or enamelled decoration, intended to contain a relic or perfume – or perhaps even poison, according to the sinister tales of the Borgias. In the case of *memento mori* rings, designed to remind the wearer of his or her mortality, there might be a tiny enamelled gold skeleton concealed within. Many such rings appear quite conventional at first glance, with only a discreet hinge fitting at the side of the bezel to indicate their complex nature. Gimmel rings (from   70 the Latin *gemellus*, twin), made of two interlocking bands, were frequently used as wedding rings, their construction symbolizing the uniting of two people in marriage. They were often combined with the *fede* motif of clasped hands, and might have a quotation from the marriage service engraved on the inner surfaces of the bands.

With changing fashions in headdresses and hairstyles, earrings became popular once again after an absence in most European countries of several centuries. Portraits from the court of Elizabeth I indicate a fashion for earrings from the 1580s onwards, when they were worn by the men – including Sir Walter Raleigh and Elizabeth's French suitor the Duke of Alençon – as well as the ladies of the court. Most are simple pear-shaped pearls or jewelled drops which were either fixed in pierced ears or tied to

70 This German gimmel ring from the late 16th century, of silver-gilt set with gemstones, has words from the marriage service engraved on the inside surfaces: 'What God hath joined together let not man put asunder.'

71, 72 The Drake Jewel, an elaborate pendant given by Queen Elizabeth I to Sir Francis Drake probably after the defeat of the Spanish Armada in 1588. The front has a sardonyx cameo in an enamelled gold frame set with table-cut rubies and diamonds. The back, set with rubies, opens to reveal a miniature of the Queen by Nicholas Hilliard, and a phoenix painted on parchment within the lid.

the ear by a length of ribbon. More elaborate examples include single jewelled letters, blackamoors, dolphins and mermaids. Earrings of the early 17th century have geometric rather than figurative designs, and tend to be longer. A more unusual development was the fashion for earstrings – fine silk cords attached to a plain hoop in the ear, which hung down to around shoulder length with a small pendant at the end. Bracelets were revived in the late 16th century after an even longer

75

73 The Ermine Portrait of Queen Elizabeth I, attributed to William Segar, 1585 (detail). Amongst her many jewelled clasps and pearls, she wears the Three Brothers pendant on her bodice. This famous 15th-century jewel (see p. 79) consisted of three large rubies, a square diamond, and pearls.

absence. They were usually worn in pairs, and were made either of close-linked chain with a rectangular enamelled clasp, or from a string of pearls or beads.

72, 73   Elizabeth I's love of jewelry was legendary, and she is always portrayed wearing an impressive array including necklaces, pendants, brooches, dress ornaments, chains, rings, and jewels in her hair. Her clothes too were often scattered with pearls, although these were not always real. Many pieces had been inherited from her father, some were the gifts of foreign ambassadors, and large numbers were presented to her as New Year gifts by members of the nobility (at New Year in 1587 she received eighty such gifts). The Queen gave jewels to reward distinguished service,
71, 72   and the pendants given to men such as Sir Francis Drake and Sir Thomas Heneage are amongst the finest surviving jewels of the period. Elaborately decorated with enamel and perhaps a sardonyx cameo, some also contained a miniature of Elizabeth by Nicholas Hilliard. Emblems and conceits, where an image was used to represent an idea, were of great importance in Elizabethan jewelry. Jewelled frogs became a popular theme when the Duke of Alençon, whose nickname was 'Frog', was paying court to the Queen. More complex emblematic pieces might have a secret political message, such as the enigmatic Lennox Jewel which incorporates twenty-eight emblems and six inscriptions. Its full meaning remains a mystery, but it is thought to have been commissioned by the Countess of Lennox, mother of Lord Darnley, as a means of conveying politically dangerous information to her husband after his return to Scotland. More conventional conceits were taken from contemporary books of emblems.

The difficult technique of enamelling on glass, known as *émail en résille sur verre*, was developed at the beginning of the 17th century and used to make cases for miniatures. The coloured glass body was first engraved with the design and the areas of pattern hollowed out. These were lined with gold foil and filled with powdered enamel of different colours, then the piece was fired. The process created vivid, luminous colours but was too intricate to become widespread.

Distinctive of the first decades of the 17th century is the creation of pattern using the actual stones, with the goldwork receding to provide
75   merely the framework or setting. The surviving sketchbook of the Dutch jeweller Arnold Lulls, who worked at the court of James I of England, shows large table-cut stones in simple formal settings with very little enamelled gold decoration in between. Geometric clusters or lines of diamonds forming initial letters and emblematic motifs were fashionable. Typically the backs of these pieces were decorated in what was known as

74 Enamelled gold chains, some set with gemstones, from the early 17th century. A wide variety of patterned chains was available throughout the Renaissance, but because of their fragility they rarely survive. These examples, from the Cheapside Hoard, are thought to have been part of a London goldsmith's stock (see p. 96).

75 Earrings of diamonds, emeralds and pearls, from the album of jewelry drawings by Arnold Lulls, a Dutch goldsmith at the court of James I of England. Dating from *c.* 1610, they show pattern now defined by the shapes and arrangement of the stones, rather than by an elaborate sculpted gold setting.

black ornament, where a scrolling pattern of strapwork was drawn in the gold, silhouetted against a black enamel background. A number of little jewels might be tied by ribbon bows to the standing lace collars of the period: those of James's wife, Anne of Denmark, included the diamond-set initials of her mother and brother, and a diamond crossbow. Less jewelry was now worn by men, usually only rings, chains, the badge of a chivalric or religious order, and sometimes a portrait miniature. James I, however, continued to wear large jewels in his hat, such as the Three Brothers and the Mirror of Great Britain, made of three large diamonds and a ruby, which was commissioned to symbolize the Union of the Kingdoms in 1604.

94

76 Bodice ornament in the *cosse-de-pois* style, of enamelled gold and diamonds, made in France or the Netherlands *c.* 1630. The pattern of tapering, curling leaves around a central rosette is picked out in rows of table-cut diamonds. The piece is constructed of three layers which are joined together with small gold screws.

76   In the 1620s a new, rather more naturalistic manner in jewelry design emerged in Paris, with a type of pattern based on stylized foliage and swirling pea-pods, and accordingly known as *cosse-de-pois*. It was used to decorate flat surfaces such as cases for miniatures, when it was drawn in
76   two contrasting colours of enamel. Extravagant diamond bodice ornaments and aigrettes for the hair were also made in this style, although these are less common. Rows of table-cut diamonds were used to outline the arching, tapering leaves (which are symmetrical in bodice ornaments, and asymmetrical in aigrettes), while the new rose-cut stones were incorporated as flowers. A large bodice ornament in this style is depicted in Rubens' portrait of his second wife Hélène Fourment, painted *c.* 1630.

A major collection of early 17th-century jewelry of a slightly more modest kind was discovered in London in 1912 as a result of demolition work. Known as the Cheapside Hoard, it is thought to have belonged to a jeweller and pawnbroker who for some reason concealed his stock in around 1630. While some of the pieces would have been very costly, much would have been intended for rich merchants' wives. The hoard
74   includes gold chains with enamelled flower-shaped links, rings with enamelled bands and bezels of cabochon emeralds in cluster settings, pendants shaped as bunches of emerald and amethyst grapes hanging on fine gold wires, and cascades of faceted amethyst drops set in delicate enamelled gold frameworks. There are also two watches (including one set within a large hexagonal emerald), engraved gems and paste imitations, hat ornaments, hairpins and buttons. Some of the pieces look back to the late 16th century, but most have the new restrained settings which give full prominence to the stones, and show the diffusion of fashions from the court to the middle classes.

77 The Scottish aristocrat Margaret Hamilton is seen *c.* 1638 wearing strings of pearls at her neck and threaded through her hair, and large pearl drops as earrings. The panels of her satin gown are held in place by substantial jewelled clasps. This detail comes from a portrait of her with her husband, Lord Belhaven, from the studio of Van Dyck.

CHAPTER FIVE

Baroque to Revolution

The early 17th century witnessed the waning of Spanish influence over European court life, and the emergence of the French as the leaders of style. During the previous century the Habsburg rulers of Spain and Austria had dominated the diplomatic scene, and their marriage alliances had encouraged a unity in court dress and jewelry throughout Europe. The French under Louis XIII now came to play an increasingly powerful role in European politics, and this growing diplomatic strength was accompanied by an influence over court fashions and manners. By the 1630s heavily embroidered and jewelled farthingales had been exchanged for flowing gowns with puffed sleeves and low necklines, and hair was arranged less severely in soft shoulder-length ringlets. This new look is familiar to us from the paintings of Rubens and Van Dyck.   77

Quantities of pearls were worn with these new, softer styles, and indeed for a short time they appear to have supplanted other materials almost completely. In general there was an increased emphasis on massed gemstones arranged in abstract symmetry rather than the sculpted and enamelled figures of earlier settings. Botany became a favourite source of

styles and fashions. This is particularly valuable as so much 17th- and 18th-century jewelry has been lost, re-set by later generations.

The Spanish were slow to accept the Baroque designs coming out of France. Their main types continued to be inspired by religion – pendant crosses, reliquaries, or symbols of the Inquisition and the Order of Santiago. Such pieces were common to both men and women, as were the intricate, long gold chains worn over one shoulder and across the chest, which had been in fashion since the second half of the 16th century. When they did finally adopt the Baroque style shortly before 1700, it remained popular for another century.

Archaeological explorations of shipwrecked Spanish galleons have revealed that in the 17th century the Spanish were importing European-style jewelry from the Philippines, evidence of a surprising degree of cross-fertilization between East and West at this date. The galleon *Nuestra Señora de la Concepción* sank in 1638 between Manila and Acapulco with a cargo of decorated gold mesh chains and filigree buttons intended for the European market. It is thought that they were made in the Philippines in workshops where Chinese craftsmen were overseen by Spanish goldsmiths. The recovery of these datable pieces is particularly significant as, although they often appear in portraits, few have survived.

80

79 *opposite* Anonymous ring designs from the second quarter of the 17th century. The sculpted and enamelled shoulders illustrate various themes including love and death; and a choice of pointed, cabochon, table-cut or rose-cut stones is offered.

80 Intricate gold chains remained fashionable longest in Spain. They are seen here worn across one shoulder by the Infanta Margarita Maria of Austria, in a detail of her portrait by Diego Velásquez, *c.* 1659. Her bodice ornament and earrings are emphasized by fabric trimmings.

Being easily damaged and without enamel or gemstones they were the most likely items to be melted down for their monetary value.

English jewelry in the mid-17th century was more affected by the Civil War than by Continental fashions, particularly during the years of Puritanism under Oliver Cromwell. Following the execution of Charles I in 1649 many commemorative pieces were made for surreptitious Royalist wear, some even claiming to contain a lock of hair or a fragment of the King's blood-soaked shirt as a relic. They ranged from inexpensive silver lockets stamped with the head of the 'Martyr King' to fine gold and enamel jewels, often with concealed double portraits of Charles I and the future Charles II. Similar jewelry was later made in support of James II and Bonnie Prince Charlie, but this was less plentiful.

Even wedding rings attracted Puritan hostility in England during the Commonwealth, but they went on being worn, ranging in style from plain gold bands to enamelled and gem-set rings; the custom of engraving a blessing or promise of fidelity on the inside continued, and books such as *The Mysteries of Love or the Arts of Wooing* (1658) gave appropriate phrases or 'posies' from which to choose. More elaborate rings were made throughout the 17th century. These included both

81

single stones and clusters of small gems such as rose-cut diamonds arranged in a geometric pattern or encircling a larger coloured stone.

81   Various forms of *memento mori* jewelry were current throughout Europe, encouraged by wars and plagues. Like those of the 16th century, they were decorated with death's heads, skeletons and coffins – the iconography of death – and were intended to encourage virtuous living. Jewelry commemorating the death of a particular person emerged during the second half of the 17th century. It usually consisted of a panel of woven hair on which the deceased's initials, coat of arms and date of death were worked in fine gold wire; a small skeleton or winged hour-glass of enamelled gold was sometimes added. The composition was then covered with a piece of faceted crystal and set as a ring or a slide to be worn on a ribbon at the neck or wrist.

The marked increase in the use of diamonds indicates that these stones were becoming more easily available in Europe. The traveller and merchant Jean-Baptiste Tavernier (1605–89) journeyed several times to India, visiting the celebrated mines at Golconda, and returning with stones of the finest quality. The brilliant cut – which remains the most popular shape for diamonds – made its first appearance in the later decades of the 17th century. Closely related to the table cut, it is deeper and enhanced with 33 facets around the top or crown and 25 around the bottom or pavilion. It probably originated in Paris, although Amsterdam became the commercial centre for diamond cutting. By the end of the century, it was common practice for diamonds to be backed with foil to enhance their sparkle, and to be set in silver rather than gold, to augment the illusion of size and emphasize the whiteness of the stones.

82–84, 86   The bow was one of the most popular motifs in Baroque jewelry, probably developing out of the ribbons which were tied at the top of a jewel as a means of securing it. Examples crowning pendants, brooches and earrings are particularly noticeable in portraits from the middle of the century. They are usually decorated with table- and rose-cut stones on the front and painted enamel on the reverse. Versions with long,

82 *above* This detail from a Dutch
family portrait of 1662 demonstrates
how bows were a universally popular
motif – either made of ribbon with a
jewel hanging below, as worn by the
daughters, or with both parts of
diamonds, as worn by the mother.

83, 84 *right* Two views of a Sévigné
of enamelled gold set with gemstones
and pearls, closely related to designs
by Gilles Légaré and François
Lefebvre from the 1660s. The back
has painted enamel flowers.

81 *opposite* Mourning and *memento
mori* rings of the 17th century:
(back row) English loyalist rings – one
commemorating the executed King
Charles I, his miniature within a
frame of diamonds, the other set with
woven hair and the initials of King
Charles II and Catherine of Braganza
in gold wire; (front row) gold rings
decorated with enamelled skulls and
crossbones, popular reminders of man's
mortality throughout Western Europe;
these late 17th-century examples are
also set with diamonds or rubies.

downward-curving loops came to be known as 'Sévignés' after the French writer Madame de Sévigné. Bows were also prominent in the ribbon-like necklaces and bracelets made of linked loops and knots of enamelled gold.

Towards the end of the century, the Brandenburg came into fashion. Like the Sévigné it was a long horizontal brooch, but with a more compact arrangement of stones, and it tapered at each end. Based on the ornate fastenings of Prussian military uniforms, it had been introduced as a jewel for men by the Duc d'Orléans in 1677, but was soon adopted by women at the French court as an alternative to the Sévigné. Several matching brooches might be worn together, arranged down the bodice according to size. The backs by now were usually engraved.

As the 18th century approached, the mounts of gem-set jewelry became more delicate, giving greater prominence to the splendour of the closely packed stones. This can be seen in extravagant Spanish bodice ornaments, often with matching earrings, which make full use of the gold and emeralds from Central and South America. Such examples have often survived because they were presented to shrines and churches.

Fashions in earrings kept pace with the rest of jewelry, and although simple pearl drops remained popular particularly in Britain, on the Continent new and more complex earrings were being worn. Portraits from the 1650s onwards show women wearing large ornaments in two or three sections, which reflected the patterns of larger pieces and were likewise made of gold, gemstones and painted enamel. Bows and flowers were often featured, but the most typical form by 1700, and on throughout the greater part of the 18th century, was the girandole. Named after contemporary candelabra hung with crystal pendants, such earrings consisted of three drops, set with the central one slightly lower, attached to the upper section by a bow or knot.

Men wore jewelry throughout the 17th century, although it was increasingly confined to special occasions. It was at its most extravagant in France under Louis XIV, whose splendid collection of diamonds included stones from the English Crown jewels bought by Cardinal Mazarin at the time of the Civil War. He delighted in diamond buttons, and buckles for garters and shoes, and in 1685 alone his jeweller supplied him with 118 diamond buttons. In England men were more restrained, although Van Dyck's portrait of Charles I on horseback shows him wearing a pearl drop in his ear, and he is known to have had a large collection of pearl buttons. Men wore the least jewelry in Spain, where they were officially restricted to neck chains and hat badges, sometimes with the addition of chivalric orders or religious pendants.

85 Louis XIV had an extensive collection of diamonds, many of which he wore
as buttons. These were made in sets of over a hundred, and can be seen here
stitched all over his brocade coat.

86 Necklace of enamelled gold bows set with table-cut diamonds and with a large pearl and sapphire drop, probably French, *c.* 1660. The gold loops at the ends are for ribbons which would tie at the back of the neck.

87 A typical Spanish bodice ornament, c. 1700. It is made of gold and emeralds from the New World, together with diamonds; enamelled flowers and stylized insects set on springs would quiver as the wearer moved.

Louis XV of France, who reached his majority in 1723, was to set a lighthearted and elegant court style which would be imitated by princes and kings all over Europe. The importance of diamonds and precious stones continued, and pieces of extraordinary splendour were created. At the same time high-quality imitation or paste jewelry was made. Design moved gradually away from cluster settings to the more flowing naturalism and exuberant ribbon bows that were to remain important until the 1780s. Asymmetrical bouquets or individual flowers were 90 confected of gold and diamonds. Enamel decoration was now only used in the most conservative circles, notably in Spain, and the backs of pieces were generally left plain. Although France still set the fashions, there was immense wealth and patronage in other parts of Europe, particularly in St Petersburg, Dresden, Lisbon and London. As the century progressed a clear division emerged between jewelry appropriate for daytime and the more opulent pieces reserved for evening wear.

90 In this Russian bouquet of brilliant-cut diamond flowers and emerald stems, of *c.* 1760, the soft colours of the flowers are achieved by setting coloured foils behind the diamonds.

91 *Giardinetti* – 'little garden' – rings, of gold set with diamonds, rubies, emeralds, amethysts and pastes in silver collets. The type was popular throughout Western Europe in the 1740s and 1750s.

92 Opaline paste jewelry set in silver, including girandole earrings, necklace and buttons, probably French, *c.* 1760. The 'opals' are made by laying a pink foil behind milky blue glass.

achieved were ideal for the romantic naturalism of the period, while the use of the brilliant cut ensured that the stones sparkled well by candle-light. Madame de Pompadour (1721–63) had a parure in which the diamonds had been foiled to tint them pale pink, green and yellow, and magnificent bouquets made of variously coloured foiled diamonds have survived in Russian collections. These flower jewels could be worn on the bodice or in the hair and were often augmented by birds and butter-flies on wires or springs which shimmered and glittered in the light as the wearer moved.

Diamond jewelry for the hair typically consisted of a single large asymmetrically placed ornament known as an aigrette, which might be in the form of a bunch of flowers, ears of wheat or a feather. Necklaces of the 1760s were worn high on the neck, usually either a simple row of pearls or else a jewelled garland of ribbons and flowers intertwined, often with a matching pendant and sometimes with a lower loop known as an esclavage. They were fastened at the back by silk ribbons attached to metal loops. Miniatures in jewelled frames were worn as brooches, or mounted as bracelet clasps which fastened multiple strands of pearls.

93 A German stomacher brooch of brilliant-cut diamonds and pearls set in silver-gilt, c. 1710–20. Made in two parts to allow movement, it filled the whole front panel of the bodice.

94 *opposite* Three diamond bow-shaped brooches which would have been worn down the front of the bodice, shown together with six from a set of forty-six shuttle-shaped dress ornaments, designed to be stitched all over the gown; Russian, c. 1760–70.

Diamond brooches were often large, and the entire front panel of a bodice from the neckline to the waist was covered by the stomachers of the middle decades of the century, which were usually made in connecting sections to allow movement. A series of matching brooches, often bow-shaped, descending in size towards the waist was a popular alternative to the stomacher. Gowns might also be scattered with precious stones made into buttons and dress ornaments and perhaps with a diamond-encrusted border along the hem. (A collection of forty-six shuttle-shaped diamond dress ornaments from *c.* 1770 has survived from the Russian Crown jewels.) On a less lavish scale, small flower brooches were used to pin up the overskirts of court dresses and also to decorate the sleeves. After Halley's comet appeared in 1758, stylized comets

93

94

94

became a popular alternative to flowers. The most frequently worn style of earring remained the girandole.

91   The fashion for flower designs was captured in miniature by the *giardinetti* rings of the mid-century, which have tiny baskets of flowers made from coloured gemstones and rose-cut diamonds in delicate open-work settings. Other styles of ring have bezels decorated with sculpted and enamelled figures, such as a carnival mask or blackamoor's head, which often conceal a secret compartment.

Neo-Classical elements began to appear as early as the 1760s, co-existing with the still popular naturalistic bouquets and ribbons of recent decades. Floral garlands remained a popular theme but arrangements became increasingly regular and ordered, characterized by delicacy rather than wild profusion. The French court of Louis XVI (reigned 1774–92) and Marie-Antoinette was less extravagant than that of Louis XV, although pieces on a lavish scale were commissioned right up to the end of the *ancien régime*: Marie-Antoinette, for example, ordered a diamond bouquet of wild roses and hawthorn blossom from Bapst in 1786. Festoon necklaces, which formed a glittering tracery of diamonds over the bosom, and filled the low necklines of court dresses, were amongst the most fashionable jewels of the 1770s and 1780s.

95   The most notorious item of jewelry of the 1770s was a diamond festoon necklace of immense value – 1,600,000 *livres* – that Louis XV had commissioned for his mistress Madame du Barry, which became the focus of a scandal surrounding Marie-Antoinette. Louis XV had died before it was completed and paid for, and the Court jewellers Böhmer and Bassenge tried unsuccessfully to sell it to Louis XVI. Eventually in 1785 a devious plan to steal the necklace was set in motion by the Comtesse de La Motte, who convinced the Cardinal de Rohan, an unwitting accomplice, that the Queen wished to acquire it without her husband's knowledge. The Cardinal bought it on her behalf, but was further deceived, for the necklace was carried to England and was broken up. When the story came out, people were all too ready to believe in Marie-Antoinette's extravagance, and it contributed significantly to revolutionary discontent in Paris.

Men were extravagantly adorned in the mid-18th century. In his Memoirs Giovanni Jacopo Casanova (1725–98) talks of his snuff box, diamond and ruby watch chain and his rings which, as typical accessories of the period, made him appear a convincing nobleman. Diamond buttons made of clusters of stones remained one of the most versatile ornaments. On a larger scale there were jewelled badges for orders of chivalry and societies, and amongst the Catholic nobility of Europe the

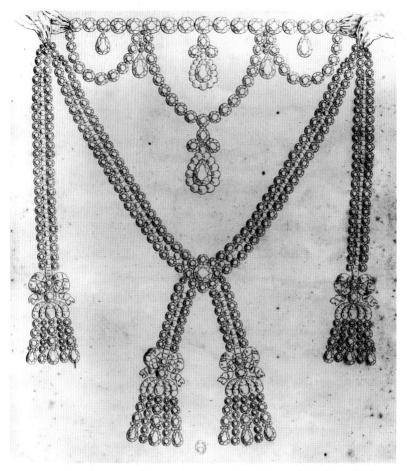

95 The ill-fated festoon necklace at the centre of the Diamond Necklace Affair. Commissioned from Böhmer and Bassenge by Louis XV in the 1770s for his mistress Madame du Barry, it contained 647 brilliant-cut diamonds, totalling 2,800 carats in weight. It was broken up, but its notoriety led to its recording in several engravings.

Order of the Golden Fleece continued to inspire elaborate badges. Even the middle classes developed their equivalent decorations, such as that of the Anti-Gallican Society in England which had been founded around 1745 to promote British manufactures and discourage importing of French goods. Gentlemen wore shoebuckles and stock buckles (to fasten high cravats at the back of the neck), which in court circles might be set with diamonds. Few examples of such jewelry have survived, as most was broken up in the 19th century when men's costume became more austere. In the late 18th century seals set as rings were supplanted by mounted seals hanging from a fob or watch chain. The fob, which was originally the small pocket in the waistband of a gentleman's trousers in which he kept his watch, came to refer to the chain itself, and eventually to the ornaments hanging from it. As chains were still made by hand, they remained costly items; alternatives to gold included woven hair. On the Continent ornaments were more elaborate, and English travellers in the 1790s were surprised to see men in France and Italy wearing earrings.

92 Non-precious materials such as paste and cut steel reached very high levels of design and craftsmanship, and were even worn at court. In paste jewelry the glass stones are cut and polished like diamonds and then mounted individually in foiled closed-back silver settings. As early as the 1670s George Ravenscroft of London had pioneered a type of flint glass made with lead oxide, which was hard enough to be faceted. However this was improved by Georges-Frédéric Strass (1701–73), who produced the most enduring form of paste. In 1734 he was appointed jeweller to Louis XV, and his fame was such that in France paste has been known as *strass* ever since. Paste stones were also produced in Venice and Bohemia, but Paris remained the main centre for imitation jewelry, and in 1767 the formal corporation of Bijoutiers-Faussetiers numbered over three hundred craftsmen.

With paste the designer had fewer constraints than he would have had if setting real diamonds, as a wider range of sizes and shapes was possible and affordable. Other stones too were imitated in glass, for a variety of colours could be made depending on the metal oxide added. Imitation opals were achieved by setting unfaceted milky blue glass over a pink foil. Paste parures have a particular interest as records of settings: the regular re-mounting of family gems has meant that most examples of real diamond jewelry from the 18th century have not survived, whereas these, with their low intrinsic value, were less likely to be altered or broken up when fashions changed.

96 Cut steel, made into faceted beads and studs or pierced to form flat sequins and decorative chain links, was exported from England all over Europe. Such work had been produced in Woodstock near Oxford since the early 17th century, and from the 1760s the industry spread to London, Birmingham and Wolverhampton. Most of the jewelry is made from faceted studs arranged in patterns, closely packed to increase their sparkle, and riveted or screwed onto a steel backplate – suggesting that the technique was originally developed by blacksmiths rather than jewellers. In contrast marcasite jewelry, which created similar effects with

96 Cut steel buckles and buttons set with blue jasper-ware plaques by Wedgwood, probably made at Matthew Boulton's Soho Works, Birmingham, c. 1785–95. Both materials, originally English specialities, became widely popular on the Continent in the late 18th century.

crystals of iron pyrites, used conventional collets. Both were combined with other materials such as blister pearls and ceramic or enamel plaques. Particularly successful was the marriage of cut steel with jasper-ware cameos from Josiah Wedgwood (see p. 120), which was pioneered by the Birmingham manufacturer Matthew Boulton. Cut steel featured prominently in the 'Anglomania', or passion for all things English, which swept Continental fashions in the 1780s. Its popularity survived the French Revolution and it was worn by both Napoleon's empresses, but by then English manufacturers were facing growing European competition, particularly from France.

96

Semi-precious stones were much used for pieces worn during the day. Garnets were fashionable for most of the century; cut thinly, foiled and set in gold, they were perhaps at their prettiest in the flower and ribbon designs of the 1750s and 1760s. Moss agate (also known as moco- or mocha-stone) with its delicate fern-like veining also enjoyed a long popularity. It was set into bracelets and buttons, as well as rings. In her collection of over forty rings Madame de Pompadour had several with moss agates surrounded by diamonds. Others were set with malachite, moonstone and carbuncle (unfaceted garnet), stones which greatly added to the colours possible in less formal jewelry.

The most important item of daytime jewelry for women during the 18th century was the chatelaine, or équipage as it was then called. It originated as a means of attaching a watch and key to the wearer's belt. By the 1720s other elements had been added and its decorative potential was firmly established. Most consisted of a central decorative plaque or series of plaques which hooked on to a belt and supported items including a matching watch, a seal and an étui (a small case containing miniature tools such as a bodkin, scissors, pencil, ivory writing tablet and a folding fruit-knife). The panels were well suited to figurative decoration, and many featured scenes from Classical mythology – either chased or cast in the gold, or by the 1770s minutely painted in enamel. One of the finest exponents of both gold-chasing and enamelling was George Michael Moser (1706–83), a Swiss craftsman working in London, who made chatelaines and watch-cases. Cheaper models were cast in pinchbeck, a gold-coloured alloy of zinc and copper invented some time before 1732 by Christopher Pinchbeck, a London watch-maker. Alternatively they were made from panels of hardstones such as bloodstone or agate set in gold scrollwork. Towards the end of the century the basic shape changed to a more delicate arrangement known as a 'macaroni' or hookless chatelaine. This consisted of enamelled chains which hung over the wearer's belt, the ends descending in equal length

97

97 Chatelaines were both decorative and functional. This example has a scissors case flanked by a needle case on the left, an étui on the right, and two thimble cases. It is English, of *c.* 1735, and made of pinchbeck.

on either side with the usual accessories attached. To balance the watch, a *fausse montre* or watch-shaped locket was often attached at the other end. By around 1800 chatelaines began to fall out of use.

Shoe buckles were a widespread element of day-time jewelry, worn by both men and women. They made their appearance early in the century, replacing laces or ribbons, and were initially small and simply decorated. Soon they tended to become more ornate, and to incorporate a wide variety of materials ranging from diamonds via paste, cut steel and blued steel to black japanned tin for mourning. In size they varied over the years, reaching their largest in the 1770s when they covered the whole instep. Buckles remained an essential part of fashionable dress until *c.* 1790.

Cameos and to a lesser extent intaglios were a major element of the Neo-Classical style (see below, pp. 126-27). British craftsmen and manufacturers produced cheaper alternatives that were fashionable in their own right, such as Bilston enamel medallions painted with Classical heads, and ceramic and glass imitation cameos. From the 1770s, Josiah Wedgwood produced distinctive jasper-ware plaques with white figures set against a coloured background for use in jewelry: these became very popular, and were later copied in hard-paste porcelain by the factories at Sèvres in France and Meissen in Germany. Glass cameos were made by James Tassie of Glasgow and his nephew William, using moulds taken from famous collections of antique and contemporary engraved gems. They offered an immense choice (15,000 different examples were listed by 1791), and many were bought by specialist collectors, including the Russian Empress Catherine the Great who ordered a complete set, as well as by those wishing to use them in rings.

Mourning rings conformed to standard types in 18th-century Britain: during the second quarter, a discreet band, often divided into five or six curling scrolls, was common – decorated with black enamel for those who were married and white for the unmarried, and inscribed in gold letters with the name, age and date of death. From the 1760s until the end of the century, miniature compositions featuring urns, broken pillars, willows, weeping maidens in Classical dress and other restrained funerary images were painted in sepia on ivory or vellum, often incorporating tiny seed pearls and hair. They were set under glass with a compartment for a lock of hair, and the name and dates of the deceased engraved on the reverse. The rings are particularly distinctive, with elongated oval or rectangular bezels that cover most of the finger up to the knuckle, although the panels were also set in brooches and lockets. Money was usually left for the purchase of these memorials in the deceased's will.

Rings and lockets set with painted ivory scenes were also given as love tokens, in this case depicting symbols such as cupids, doves, and hearts aflame on an altar. Locks of curled or woven hair were set behind crystal, often framed with half pearls, garnets or enamel. Those shaped as padlocks and keys represented the key to the wearer's (or giver's) heart, and those framed by a serpent biting its tail symbolized eternity. Portrait medallions remained very popular for bracelet clasps, pendants and rings, and silhouette portraits, which were less expensive, were introduced

96

98

98 Amatory lockets, of enamelled gold, glass, mother-of-pearl and seed pearls: (top) depicting a pair of doves drinking at a fountain, inscribed 'L'Amour et l'Amitié' (love and friendship), with Paris hallmarks for 1797–1809; (left) set with a miniature of a woman with a dove and a crane, converted from a bracelet clasp, possibly English, late 18th century; (right) showing an altar inscribed 'A Vous Dédié' (dedicated to you), with hearts aflame and doves carrying a garland of flowers, French, late 18th century; (bottom) in the form of a padlock with a pendant heart and key representing the key to one's heart, English, c. 1800.

from the 1770s. Amatory jewelry was worn by men, usually concealed beneath a shirt or attached to a watch fob, as well as by women. Enigmatic portrait miniatures showing just a finely painted eye spread from France in the mid 1780s. They were thought to be a more discreet and teasing variant on the portrait, leaving the identity of the sitter a mystery.

The ring remained one of the most popular of sentimental jewels, and amatory messages were conveyed in a variety of ways. Letters might be arranged on the bezel as decorative rebuses, such as 'M MOI' for *aimes moi* (love me) and 'JM' for *j'aime* (I love). Gimmel or connecting twin rings were still worn: the Prince of Wales gave one to Mrs Fitzherbert at their morganatic marriage in 1785, inscribed on the inner surfaces with their names. Other rings used for weddings included diamond hoops, half hoops and clusters of stones arranged as two crowned hearts.

CHAPTER SIX

Empire, Historicism and Eclecticism

The making and wearing of jewelry in France was interrupted dramatically by the Revolution in 1789, before re-emerging with the magnificent Neo-Classical creations of the First Empire. Despite this hiatus the French managed to retain their role as the leaders of high fashion, and such was their influence that even during the long period of hostilities between 1793 and 1815 Parisian styles were avidly followed in London.

At the outbreak of the Revolution jewelry, which was such a potent symbol of the monarchy and court, suffered a dramatic reversal of fortune. Its possession indicated aristocratic status, and during the Terror even a pair of fancy shoe buckles might be enough to condemn their owner to the guillotine. Those who supported or hoped to appease the revolutionaries gave their jewelry to the cause, while others hid their jewels or took them as financial security when they fled. With the sales that followed – which eventually included some of the French Crown jewels – the European market became flooded with stones and prices fell. Meanwhile in Paris the only acceptable adornments were crude commemorative pieces, some made from stone or metal fragments of the Bastille. Most common were simple iron rings inscribed with patriotic phrases celebrating its storming, or stamped with portrait busts of heroes such as Marat.

99

99 Ideologically acceptable jewelry: this roughly mass-produced ring of silver commemorates the revolutionary heroes Jean Paul Marat and Louis Michel Lepelletier de Saint Fargeau, both murdered in 1793. Versions of the ring were also made in iron.

123

The Paris Company of Goldsmiths, abolished in 1791, was reinstated in 1797, and some of the jewellers from the reign of Louis XVI re-opened. In 1798, ahead of the rest of Europe, France introduced compulsory hallmarking for jewelry. Gold was divided into three standards of purity – 750, 840 and 920 parts per 1000 – and pieces were stamped with a maker's mark which consisted of the maker's or sponsor's initials and symbol in a lozenge-shaped punch. At first craftsmen were handicapped by the general shortage of money and materials, and this gave rise to delicate, flimsy goldwork. Much of it was inspired by traditional French peasant jewelry, using filigree, seed pearls and modest stones, particularly cornelian. Sautoirs (long decorated chains) were worn diagonally from the shoulder in military fashion, or simply round the neck; and long pendant earrings known as *poissardes* were fashionable.

100 Pieces showing the influence of Neo-Classicism: (top) wreath tiara (the sections are hinged) of enamelled gold set with a paste cameo, diamonds and pearls, *c.* 1810; (centre) cornelian intaglio in a simple gold pendant mount, *c.* 1807; (below) necklace of *pietre dure* panels connected by chains, French, *c.* 1805; (below left) watch in the form of a lyre, French, *c.* 1820; (below right) earrings of gold, enamel, pearls and emeralds, probably French, *c.* 1798.

101 *opposite* Napoleon's sister Princess Pauline Borghese wears a parure of engraved gems with the diamonds of the belt and bandeau arranged in Greek key design. (Detail of a portrait by Robert Lefèvre.)

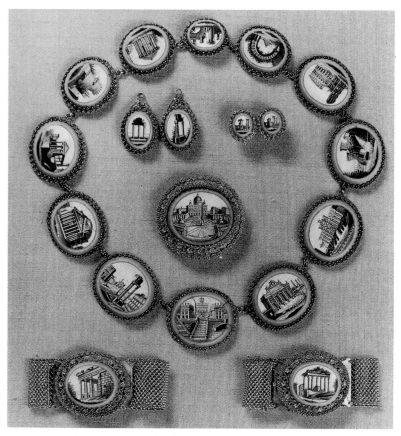

106 Parure of Italian micro-mosaic plaques depicting views of Rome. Such plaques were a popular souvenir from the Grand Tour. These have gold settings with *cannetille* decoration, made by a Parisian jeweller *c.* 1825.

106   Both Napoleon's empresses owned parures set with Italian micro-mosaic plaques, which remained fashionable throughout Europe until the mid-1870s. The mosaics were extremely laborious to produce, made from hundreds of subtly coloured tesserae cut from thin rods of opaque glass; these were arranged using tweezers on a panel of glass or copper that had been coated with mastic or cement, the gaps were filled with coloured wax, and then the surface was polished. Favourite subjects include the ruins of ancient Rome, flowers, birds and animals. These plaques were made in Italy but were usually exported unmounted and 100   set in jewelry in Paris or London. Panels of *pietre dure* ('hard stones'), sometimes known as Florentine mosaic, were popular over the same

period and were mounted in a similar way. In them the picture, typically of flowers or butterflies, was made up of thin slices of coloured hard-stone, cut and filed to shape then set into a plain marble background. The craft spread from Italy to Derbyshire, Paris and St Petersburg in the course of the century. The other important Italian contribution at this date was coral, from Naples and Sicily, which was carved into beads and cameos.

Berlin iron, made by the Royal Prussian Iron Foundry from 1804, was the most distinctive material used in German jewelry in the early 19th century. Intricate panels of scrollwork, foliage, Classical medallions and Gothic tracery were cast in very fine sand, linked together and then lacquered black. The complexity of the casting and the high standards of design (the architect Karl Friedrich Schinkel was responsible for some, including the Iron Cross medal) meant that although of base metal these pieces were expensive. The material became particularly popular for patriotic and commemorative pieces during the Prussian War of Liberation in 1812-14. Ladies were encouraged to give their gold orna-ments for the war effort and received iron in exchange. (Pieces are some-times inscribed '*Gold gab ich für Eisen*' – I gave gold for iron.) Although no longer at the forefront of fashion, it was still being made at the time of the London Great Exhibition in 1851, by which date manufacturing had spread to Austria, Bohemia and Paris. Comparatively little has survived because of its brittleness and susceptibility to rust.

107

107 Berlin iron bracelet, made by A. F. Lehmann, *c.* 1820–30. Its design combines architectural details of the Gothic Revival with naturalistic vines and foliage.

108 *above* The English Gothic Revival architect A. W. N. Pugin designed the parure which includes this headband in 1848 (see p. 142). It is made of enamelled gold, pearls, turquoises, diamonds and a ruby; the inscription translates as 'Christ's cross is my light'.

109 *below* A casket of ancient Roman-style jewelry by Castellani (see p. 138), presented by the City of Rome to Princess Maria Pia of Savoy on her marriage to King Luis I of Portugal in 1862.

110 *opposite* Crown Princess Frederick William of Prussia, painted by Heinrich von Angeli in 1882, wears a magnificent double necklace and pendant in the revived Renaissance style (see p. 144).

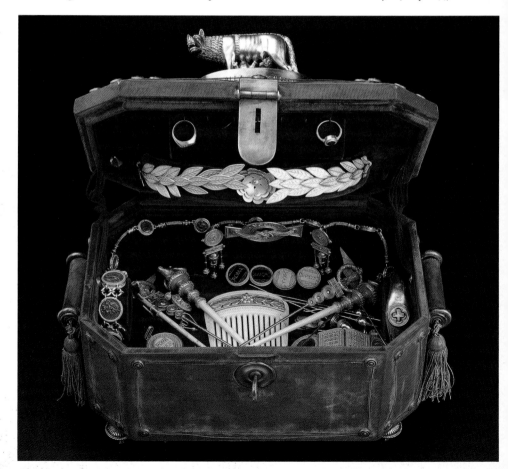

to teeth by a pivot or hinge – had appeared in France. Aigrettes, now made in coloured stones in preference to diamonds, were used particularly on turbans, while decorative combs, either of tortoiseshell or metal, 102 increasingly became the most widespread daytime hair accessory.

The usual shape for a necklace was now a single string of precious stones or pearls, often with pendant drops all round: Marie-Louise was given one in diamonds following the birth of a son, the King of Rome, in 1811, and Josephine is frequently portrayed wearing a magnificent string of pearls hung with large pear-shaped drops. As well as large single stones, clusters of diamonds around a coloured stone were also set in this style. These were fastened with sprung metal clasps, which had replaced 103 the metal loops and ribbon ties of earlier times.

The Restoration of the Bourbons in 1814 was marked by a period of relative economic austerity. Some of the Crown jewels were re-set by Bapst, this time in a style influenced by that of the 18th century to emphasize the Bourbons' link with the *ancien régime*. Few had money to buy diamonds and even at court pieces tended to be made from semi-precious stones in elaborate but thin gold mounts for maximum effect at moderate expense. Where diamonds were used they tended to be small and set in spreading collets to make them appear more substantial.

From about 1815 jewelry was made from seed pearls, which were pierced and threaded on horsehair or silk, then arranged in delicate lace-like patterns into elaborate necklaces or mounted as floral sprigs on a mother-of-pearl frame. Although laborious to thread, they were relatively inexpensive. Festoon necklaces now commonly comprised a set of cameo or mosaic plaques, linked together by strands of fine chain which 100 were carefully measured so that they fell in graceful curves. Necklaces '*à la Jeannette*' appeared in Paris in the 1820s. Thought to have originated from French regional or Huguenot christening jewelry, they consist of a black velvet ribbon with a central heart-shaped slide from which the ribbon hangs down to support a cross in gold or gold filigree.

Throughout Europe during the 1820s and 1830s contrasting multi-coloured gemstones introduced new polychrome effects. Usually the settings were encrusted with fine detailing in gold – either *cannetille*, 105, 106 where the surface is covered with spirals of wire, or *grainti*, where small granules are used. During the day, ladies took to wearing several bulky, 114 non-matching bracelets with large jewelled or portrait clasps – as many as five extending almost from the wrist to the elbow. In a similar manner numerous narrow gem-set or enamel rings were worn together on a finger. Naturalistic forms such as flowers, ears of wheat, butterflies and vines established a popularity that was to remain current for much of the

113 Stomacher from the Devonshire Parure, created by Hancocks of London in 1856 (see p. 144). Antique engraved gems are set in enamelled gold, the motif of which is copied from an Elizabethan jewel. The choice of the stomacher form is also a revival, in this case from the mid-18th century.

114 Lady Peel wears three large non-matching bracelets on her left arm, all with large jewelled clasps, and a number of rings on the same finger – a typical arrangement in 1827, when she was portrayed by Sir Thomas Lawrence.

115 *opposite* Much of the archaeological revival jewelry by Castellani was directly inspired by surviving early pieces. These gold pendants and necklace, made *c.* 1865, are close copies of originals of *c.* 360 BC, excavated from a Greek site in the Crimea.

second half of the century, and Baroque and Rococo motifs were revived. At the same time the styles of the medieval and Renaissance periods were beginning to be explored through grand costume balls in Paris and London.

Major archaeological discoveries were to have a profound effect on jewelry design from the middle of the century, re-introducing a lost repertoire of forms, ornament and techniques, all of which contributed to a new 'archaeological style'. While genuine ancient examples had occasionally been seen in society, such as the newly discovered Etruscan pieces worn by Lucien Bonaparte's wife in Rome in the 1830s, these were rare finds and tended to be of very thin gold and therefore fragile. As demand increased in the 1860s, a number of European jewellers became famous either for close copies or for freer adaptations. Their work won approval in artistic circles, where the debate as to what constituted good or appropriate design was accompanied by a reaction against precious stones and naturalistic ornament.

109, 115 The most influential firm working in the archaeological style was Castellani of Rome, established in 1814 by Fortunato Pio Castellani (1793–1865), who was followed by his two sons Alessandro (1824–83)

and Augusto (1829–1914). Through their friendship with the Duke of Sermoneta, a keen antiquarian, they kept closely in touch with discoveries and were able to amass an extensive study collection of Etruscan, Greek and Roman goldwork. Their knowledge of ancient jewelry won them an international reputation as antiquarians and restorers as well, and a visit to their shop had become an essential part of every discerning tourist's stay in Rome by the late 1850s. Their international profile was strengthened by shops in London and Paris, and by showing at the international exhibitions in Europe and America throughout the 1860s and 1870s.

Castellani's work was inspired principally by Etruscan and Greek originals which were then being excavated in Italy and the Crimea. Historical accuracy was sought, and there are many cases where it is possible to identify the model precisely. As in ancient goldwork, decoration was primarily embossed, with details in gold filigree and fine granules. Despite extensive experiments, Castellani were unable to replicate exactly the Etruscan technique of granulation but they achieved a similar effect using solder. Typical products are necklaces of woven gold wire   115 with a fringe of rosettes and hollow seed-shaped pendants. Precious stones seldom appear; colour is provided by enamel, cameos, or cornelian scarab beetles. Severe Roman-style settings were also used, usually to frame micro-mosaic copies of early Christian symbols and Byzantine mosaics, or ancient coins.

Elsewhere the archaeological style became established in the early 1860s. The Neapolitan jeweller Carlo Giuliano (d. 1895), thought to have been trained by Castellani, began working in London then, producing pieces that are technically and stylistically very similar. In France the popularity of the genre was greatly encouraged by Napoleon III's acquisition for the Louvre in 1861 of the Campana Collection, which included around twelve hundred examples of Etruscan, Greek and Roman jewelry. Eugène Fontenay (1823–87) specialized in archaeological pieces, but with less concern for historical accuracy, using diamonds and enamel plaques, and sometimes combining elements of different origin. Tiffany of New York were producing replicas of Cypriot jewelry by 1863, while the Austrian market was supplied by the Viennese firm Josef Bacher & Sohn.

Other cultures too provided inspiration. During the 1840s the Assyrian civilization became known through the discoveries of Sir Austen Henry Layard: the sculpture and friezes from the palaces at Nineveh could be seen in London at the British Museum and in Layard's illustrated accounts of the excavations. The figurative panels were re-created in gold as bracelet bands and brooches by various London jewellers during the 1850s and 1860s. Assyrian cylinder seals of carved steatite were sometimes incorporated, most splendidly in the parure Layard commissioned from Phillips in 1869 as a wedding present for his wife. (She is shown wearing it in a portrait by Vincente Palmaroli, preserved at the British Museum with the parure.) The art of ancient Egypt enjoyed renewed attention following Auguste Mariette's excavations during the 1860s and the building of the Suez canal (1854–69). Pharaonic motifs became widespread, and according to the jeweller and writer Henri Vever (1853–1942), Egyptian decoration featured in the collections of almost all the makers showing at the Paris Exhibition of 1867.

Celtic jewelry, particularly the large ring brooches of the 8th and 9th centuries, formed another aspect of the archaeological style, promoted by Dublin firms from the late 1840s onwards. After the discovery of the Tara Brooch in Ireland in 1850 G. & S. Waterhouse showed the original at the Great Exhibition in 1851 alongside cast replicas which were for sale. These and copies of other early brooches proved popular, particularly for wearing with shawls. They were usually made one-third smaller than the

116 Necklace and earrings from Lady Layard's parure, made in 1869 by Phillips of London from Assyrian cylinder seals recently excavated by her husband, set in gold mounts.

producing distinctive Renaissance-style pieces of heavily chiselled gold set with painted enamel plaques. The plaques too were a revival – of Limoges enamels of around 1500 – and were mostly made by the Sèvres factory, which had established an enamels workshop in 1845. In Germany the Renaissance Revival was characterized by a more historically exact approach based on rigorous research. The work of Reinhold Vasters of Aachen (d. 1890), who was also a restorer and prolific faker of Renaissance jewelry, is representative in its accuracy and skill.

The most ambitious English set of Renaissance- or Tudor-inspired jewelry is the Devonshire Parure, made in 1856 by C. F. Hancock for the Countess of Granville (wife of the Duke of Devonshire's nephew) to wear at the coronation of Tsar Alexander II in Moscow. Antique engraved gems from the Duke of Devonshire's collection were set, with diamonds, in a gold framework which was decorated in enamel with a colourful, symmetrical design copied from a 16th-century jewel. Such enamel-work became a distinctive element of the English Renaissance Revival, and was known as 'Holbeinesque' (a slight anachronism as the original pattern post-dated Holbein's death by almost half a century). It was widely used to frame pendants until the 1880s.

The eclecticism of 19th-century design borrowed not only from the past but also from exotic cultures which were made accessible through lavishly illustrated books like Owen Jones's *Grammar of Ornament* (published in London in 1856). The international exhibitions brought both the leading European styles and the arts and manufactures of distant continents to a very large audience, and their illustrated catalogues, which could be used as pattern books, spread the new ideas even more widely. European imperial expansion was also influential: the French conquest of Algeria in 1830 increased the interest in North African jewelry and led to the use of Islamic calligraphy as a decorative motif; while British activity in India, culminating in Queen Victoria's proclamation as Empress in 1876, made the styles of that country popular.

After two centuries of isolation Japan resumed contact with the West in the late 1850s, and at the 1862 Exhibition in London the country contributed, for the first time, a display of contemporary art and design. The Japanese had no tradition of making and wearing jewelry, but the highly developed metalworking skills of their armourers and enamellers were greatly admired. Sword mounts were traditionally made of a dark metal inlaid with gold, silver and copper. The craftsmen who specialized in that technique took to producing items of jewelry for export, especially after 1876 when the wearing of samurai swords was banned. Plaques showing figures in a landscape, birds and flowers were mounted as

118 A necklace of *cloisonné* enamel on gold by the jewellers Falize, *c.* 1867. The decoration is drawn from Japanese sources, while the distinctive enamelling technique is Chinese.

brooches and pendants. Panels of brightly coloured *cloisonné* enamel were also set in jewelry for export to Europe. The principal importer of such goods in London was Arthur Lasenby Liberty, whose influential shop opened in 1875.

The French jeweller Lucien Falize (1839–97) was particularly influenced by the Japanese exhibits in 1862, and by 1867 he and his father Alexis Falize (1811–98) had mastered the technique of Oriental *cloisonné* 118 enamel and was applying it to fine work in gold. A new vocabulary of motifs including bamboo, chrysanthemums, dragons, cranes and fans was adopted by Western designers, and by the 1870s manufacturers in Birmingham were mass-producing 'Japanese' jewelry in silver decorated with different coloured golds. An alloy of copper gave red gold; zinc, yellow gold; charcoal iron, greyish gold; whilst silver gave green or white gold depending on the proportions used.

145

119 A naturalistic brooch showing a bird on the branch of a peach tree, made of finely textured gold which has been coloured with different alloys. It is probably English, of *c.* 1850, though it could also be French.

Archaeological and exotic styles were not, of course, the only ones. The 19th century was an age of enormous variety, as designers experimented with a host of ideas and models, old and new – naturalism, humour, 'souvenir' and other themes based on association. Even established conventions, such as mourning jewelry, were not immune to changes of fashion.

Naturalistic motifs such as flowers, vines, butterflies and doves were widely popular, with sentimental meanings conventionally attached to different flowers: forget-me-nots, for instance, signified true love and lilies of the valley symbolized the return of happiness. The serpent remained a powerful and much used motif, usually depicted biting its tail to symbolize eternity. In the 1830s and 1840s such pieces were made in gold and set with coloured stones, turquoise being one of the most

120 A large diamond bodice ornament of roses, carnations and other flowers, some of which are mounted on springs to increase the sparkle as the wearer moved. The fashion was international; this piece is probably English, *c.* 1850.

fashionable. Elaborate vine-shaped necklaces have bunches of carved amethyst or seed pearl grapes set amongst chased gold or enamelled leaves. In the 1850s enormous diamond corsage ornaments of flowers 120 appeared, often with some of the blossoms on small springs so that they would tremble and glitter with the slightest movement. Coloured golds were used to create sprays, sometimes with flowers or berries carved in 119 coloured hardstone, shell or ivory. Contrasting shades of gold were chased to imitate the texture of the plant, while a finer matt surface or 'bloom' could be achieved by chemical dipping.

Humorous novelties such as cauldrons, lanterns, wheelbarrows or watering cans were much worn after around 1865. According to *The Englishwoman's Domestic Magazine*, American women in Paris in 1875 were wearing earrings shaped as steam engines, steeples, steamers and omnibuses. Novelties with animal themes include birds sitting on their nests (sometimes with pearl eggs), frogs amongst bulrushes, and insects. Reverse intaglio crystals, where a design is carved and painted in reverse into the back of a hemisphere of crystal, were made in England. Sporting jewelry, decorated with hunting scenes, horseshoes or fishing baskets, was particularly popular in England and France. Occasionally hunting trophies such as stags' teeth and lions' claws were mounted in suites, as were the iridescent green shells of South American beetles.

Styles in souvenir jewelry were slow to change, but as travel in Europe grew easier and cheaper, it became much more common. Visitors returned from Italy with pieces set with micro-mosaic or *pietre dure* panels, shell cameos and coral (pale pink was the rarest and most expensive); at Pompeii you could buy 'lava' cameos, usually decorated with classical heads, in a variety of natural shades such as dull terracotta, khaki and brown. Other typical souvenir jewelry included enamels from Switzerland and carved ivory from Dieppe in France or the Black Forest in Germany.

121   Scottish jewelry was popularized by the Romantic movement, and particularly by Queen Victoria's enthusiasm for that country. Heart-shaped 'luckenbooth' brooches, which had long been worn by poorer Scots, were now produced in more elaborate versions. Most typical are the brooches made in simple geometric forms or shaped as dirks or sporrans – as they still are today – set with local stones such as granites, agates and cairngorms (a smoky yellow quartz). By the mid-1860s, however, genuine cairngorms were being replaced by Brazilian quartz processed in the German stone-cutting centre of Idar Oberstein. With growing demand it was only a matter of time before the majority of 'Scottish' brooches were being mass-produced in Birmingham. Irish souvenirs, typically round towers, harps and shamrocks, were made of bog oak (wood which had been hardened and blackened by long submersion in peat bogs). They were usually hand carved, although after 1852 a machine could impress the design using heat and pressure, a method which gave less sharp outlines.

The etiquette surrounding death became more complex and rigid in the course of the century, with strict periods of mourning observed following a bereavement. By the 1860s a widow was expected to dress in black for a year and a day after her husband's death, wearing minimal matt black ornaments, usually of unpolished jet. Gradually she was allowed more elaborate mourning jewelry, then diamonds and pearls, and finally a return to coloured stones. Some widows, following the example of Queen Victoria, never returned to more light-hearted pieces.

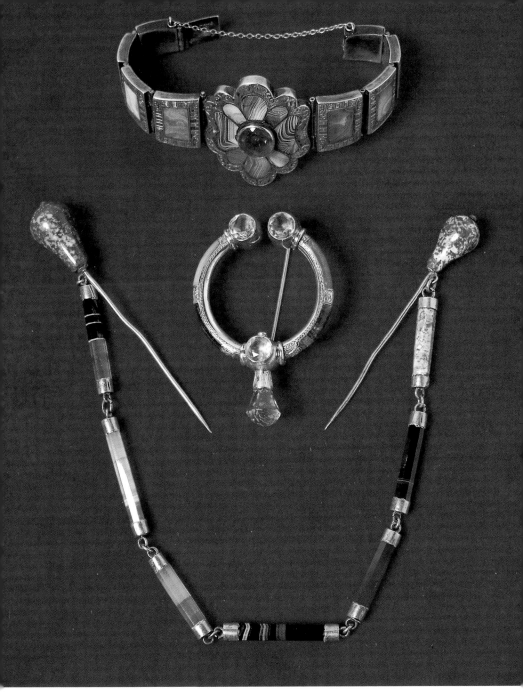

121 Scottish pebble jewelry, of silver set with different coloured agates and quartz: (from top) bracelet, *c.* 1855; shawl brooch in the form of a penannular pin, late 19th century; double scarf or shawl pin, *c.* 1845. The long popularity and traditional forms of these pieces often make them difficult to date.

The mid-19th century was a time of great scientific and mechanical advances. By the 1840s the unhealthy process of mercury-gilding, which involved heating a mixture of mercury and gold until the mercury evaporated, had been superseded by electro-gilding. A chain-making machine patented in 1859 was claimed to equal the output of seventy workers and to achieve a more even result. At around the same time prefabricated collets for stones were introduced. Safety catches and fastenings feature prominently amongst the patents relating to jewelry production: perhaps the most significant were those, beginning in the 1860s, for earring clips and screw-fastenings, which offered women an alternative to pierced ears. Crucial to the development of mass-produced jewelry was the application of steam power to stamping machines that punched out both the basic shape and the surface detailing of a piece in one rapid action.

In Britain copyright laws were introduced in 1842 which offered manufacturers protection for new patterns or technical processes which might otherwise have been copied by rival firms. Designs were registered at the Patent Office, and each piece made was then stamped with a small lozenge-shaped mark that gave in code the name of the firm and the date of registration. Although never compulsory, the system was much used by firms specializing in inexpensive jewelry, and it now identifies precisely the maker and the date of design of many otherwise anonymous pieces.

Up to the mid-19th century, virtually all Western jewelry had been designed and made in Europe. Now new areas of the world were adding their own contribution, especially America and Australia. In the United States comparatively little jewelry was worn before the mid-century. Smaller pieces such as buckles and buttons had been made by local craftsmen in centres like Boston and Providence, but most was imported from Europe. Tiffany in New York, founded in 1837 (as Tiffany & Young), initially sold only foreign goods, and their first catalogue in 1845 advertised, amongst a diverse range of goods, items such as hair ornaments and gold and imitation gold chains from London, Paris and Rome. By 1848 they had begun to produce their own gold jewelry, and were buying large quantities of diamonds in Paris, where their price had fallen due to the unstable political situation. Tiffany's importance grew rapidly and by the 1870s they had outlets in Paris, London and Geneva and were taking part in major international exhibitions.

In Australia during the early years of the century jewelry had been a luxury few could afford. There were occasional workshops set up by craftsmen who had been transported, such as Ferdinand Meurant, who

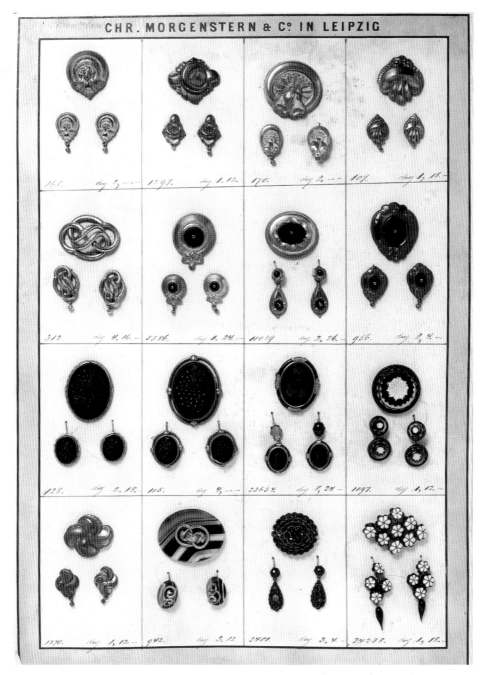

123 Inexpensive costume jewelry was mass-produced internationally, using the new steam-powered stamping machines. This card of samples by Morgenstern & Co. of Leipzig was shown at the Great Exhibition in London in 1851.

124 An Australian 'gold-field' brooch, made of gold, *c.* 1855. The figure of a miner turning a windlass is surrounded by miniature picks, shovels, a sluice box, a revolver, and other tools.

arrived around 1800 following his attempts to defraud the Bank of Ireland; but what little was sold during the first half of the century was almost all imported from Europe or second-hand. With the discovery of gold and the consequent gold rush of the 1850s and 1860s this was to change, and European-trained jewellers were attracted to the major cities. Australian themes, particularly those connected with mining, were a speciality, and 'gold-field' brooches depicting miners' tools were amongst the most characteristic novelties produced. Distinctively Australian animals, particularly kangaroos and emus, were also featured, while the Victorian interest in botany was reflected in jewelry made from quandong seeds and myall wood. Grander, more formal pieces continued to be imported from Europe.

124

CHAPTER SEVEN

The Belle Époque: Diamonds, Art Nouveau and the Arts and Crafts

Jewelry from around 1900 can be divided into three main strands. At the highest levels of privilege and wealth, particularly in the courts of Europe, lavish quantities of formal diamond jewelry continued to be worn. In style it had moved gradually away from revived Renaissance motifs to lighter forms inspired by the fashions of Louis XVI and the First Empire. Secondly, in more artistic or progressive circles in Europe the freer forms of Art Nouveau were being explored using coloured stones and enamels. Thirdly, in Britain there was a revival of traditional crafts and a reaction against mechanization. Rejecting conventional attitudes to materials and technical training, designers of the Arts and Crafts movement produced work that was characterized by the use of semi-precious stones and enamels and a hand-made look. Throughout Europe jewellers took different elements from each strand to create over-lapping national styles. Many chose semi-precious and non-precious materials for their colour and texture in preference to more valuable materials. The Paris Exhibition of 1900 was at the centre of this intensely colourful and elegant period, and the styles championed there continued with little change until the outbreak of the First World War in 1914.

Fine jewelry was almost entirely white, based on a lavish use of diamonds and pearls. The immense output of the South African diamond mines resulted in cheaper stones, and by the late 1880s over 90 per cent of Europe's diamonds came from here (although supply was temporarily interrupted by the Boer War from 1899 to 1902). Settings were made in white gold, and then increasingly in platinum – either of which gave a sympathetic white setting of greater strength than had been possible with silver.

Most typical was the delicate 'garland' style, exemplified by the designs of the Paris jeweller Cartier. It looked to pieces from the time of Louis XVI and Marie-Antoinette (original pattern books were also reprinted), and it featured garlands of laurel leaves, ribbon bows, tassels and cobweb-like trellises or lace patterns. It was a precise and elegant style, with the flowing yet restrained lines made extravagant by the concentration of

126

155

diamonds. Coloured stones were sometimes added, often peridots which were said to be Edward VII's favourite, or amethysts. Fashions in diamond jewelry were similar throughout Europe and amongst the wealthiest Americans, although botanical imagery remained strongest in Paris. By 1910 an increasingly linear approach emerged, expressed in restrained arrangements of stones. This was to be pioneered by the innovative designers of Cartier, Boucheron and Van Cleef & Arpels, and within it were the origins of Art Deco.

125 At the end of the 19th century small brooches were worn scattered in profusion all over the bodice and, with different fittings, all over the hair. Larger corsage ornaments such as 18th-century-style stomachers and jewelled swags, which framed the neckline and descended towards the waist, were also an important part of formal evening dress. Around 1910 the new, less constricting lines of Poiret's and Fortuny's dresses were complemented by a much simpler asymmetrical arrangement of two brooches linked by curving strands of diamonds, or a single large brooch which could also be worn on a headband or turban. Jewelled head ornaments, usually tiaras but also lighter aigrettes and bandeaux, remained an essential part of court and society dress in Europe and in America. Most tiaras were designed to convert into necklaces or had sections that could be detached and worn as brooches on less formal occasions. Earrings were seldom worn, but when they were they tended to be small clusters or solitaires.

125 The broad choker which fitted closely around the neck like a dog-collar was at its most fashionable around the turn of the century, encouraged by Queen Alexandra who wore one to cover a small scar on her neck. The deep band might be made of separate jewelled plaques attached to a black ribbon, of discreetly hinged metal panels, or of a central ornamental plaque flanked by multiple strings of pearls. The
126 résille necklace continued below the neck to cover the décolletage with a delicate tracery of diamonds. With the less constricting fashions of *c.* 1910, longer necklaces appeared such as the lavallière, which consisted of two overlapping diamond-set chains each with a slender jewelled pendant at the end. Long strings of pearls or amber beads were also worn.

Pearls were immensely fashionable, and remained extremely costly. Very good imitations were available, but of more lasting significance were the attempts by Kokichi Mikimoto of Japan to produce cultured pearls from the 1890s. His technique involved introducing a small bead into the oyster shell, where it would be coated in nacre as in nature. Long pearl necklaces became much more affordable, and the great rarity of large natural pearls was undermined.

125 Mrs Jay Gould, wife of
the American millionaire, in the
corseted fashions and formal
'white' jewelry typical of the
years around 1900. She wears
a tiara, diamond dog-collar
necklace, diamond and pearl
corsage ornament and ropes
of natural pearls.

126 Diamond résille necklace in
the revived Louis XVI style,
made for Queen Alexandra of
England by Cartier in 1904.

127 The Tiffany setting, devised in 1886; the diamond is supported above the band, allowing much more light into the stone, unlike earlier settings where it was partially embedded in the band.

128 *opposite* Snowflake brooch by Fabergé, made of diamonds set in platinum with a central cabochon ruby. It is shown alongside the drawing in Holmström's stockbook of a related jewel with a central ruby cross, dated 10 January 1914. The Red Cross, a cause to which the Tzarina was dedicated, recurs in Fabergé's work after the outbreak of war in 1914.

A new group of customers, wealthy industrialists and financiers, greatly stimulated the jewelry trade both in Europe and America at a time when many of the aristocratic families of Europe found their inherited wealth to be dwindling. They amassed both historic and new pieces: when the American heiress Consuelo Vanderbilt married the Duke of Marlborough in 1895 she wore pearls that had once belonged to Catherine the Great and the Empress Eugénie. Many of the wealthiest Americans chose to buy their jewelry in Paris; otherwise, Tiffany & Co. in New York were the most international and prestigious of the American firms.

At the auction of French Crown jewels in 1887, Tiffany acquired a magnificent stock of old gemstones for use in their own jewelry. At the same time they were at the forefront of discoveries of native American gemstones, and at the Paris Exhibition in 1900 were awarded a gold medal for an iris brooch made with Montana sapphires. In enamels too they produced very high quality work, including naturalistic copies of rare orchids which were also shown in 1900. Their great contribution to

127 ring design was the 'Tiffany setting', developed in 1886 for diamond solitaires. In this the gem is supported above the band of the ring by a circle of elongated claws; more light is able to pass through the stone, so that it sparkles much more brightly. It remains the standard setting used throughout much of the world today.

The most important court jeweller during this period was the Russian
128, 136 firm of Fabergé. Peter Carl Fabergé (1846–1920) had taken charge of his father's St Petersburg firm in 1870, from when its prestige throughout Russia grew steadily, overshadowing competitors such as Bolin and

Köchli, and winning an ever increasing number of imperial commissions. Most famous was the series of Easter eggs ordered each year from 1885 until the Revolution in 1917. During these years his jewelry business became the largest in the world, with an extensive workforce of designers and craftsmen. Fabergé retained close artistic control, but also acknowledged the individual genius of his workmasters by allowing them to mark their initials alongside the firm's hallmark (usually FABERGE in Cyrillic capitals). August Holmström, his son Albert Holmström, Erik Kollin and Alfred Thielemann were amongst those who specialized in jewelry.

The pieces drew their inspiration from a diversity of historical sources, but it was the 18th century, with its garlands and bows, carved hardstones and coloured golds that was the most constant. Meanwhile some designs anticipated future fashions, notably Art Deco. Miniature egg-shaped

159

128, 136 pendants were made as Easter gifts, to be worn in large numbers on necklace chains. Some of the most whimsical jewelry was of rock crystal and diamonds, forming a pattern of frost and ice crystals reminiscent of the long Russian winters.

Fabergé's workshops produced diamond jewelry of exquisite delicacy, but much of their work included less costly unconventional stones such as star sapphires, moonstones and mecca-stones (blue chalcedony usually enhanced with a pink foil). Translucent enamel, one of the firm's particular specialities, was available in almost one hundred and fifty colours. Both gold and platinum were used, but as platinum was not then hallmarked in Russia much of this work now passes unrecognized.

129–132, 137 The Art Nouveau movement has left jewelry of breathtaking subtlety and delicacy. Named after Siegfried Bing's avant-garde Paris shop 'La Maison de l'Art Nouveau', its focal point was the Paris Exhibition of 1900. Its influence was felt throughout Europe and America, where the decorative arts were transformed by extravagant swirling lines and graciously rounded forms. Sensuality was a dominant force, and images from nature were endowed with a romantic dreaminess, a world-weary melancholy or the wildness of nature uncontrolled by man. The decadence of *fin-de-siècle* Paris and the Symbolist movement's preoccupation with the exotic and the occult sometimes inspired jewelry of a more night-marish and macabre aspect.

The greatest jeweller working in this style was the Frenchman René Lalique (1860–1945). Calouste Gulbenkian began to amass his collection of around 145 major pieces in 1895, but a more general and international recognition followed the Paris Exhibition of 1900 where Lalique was awarded a *Grand Prix*. Over the following decade he produced jewelry of great originality and exquisite craftsmanship, drawing on both the beauty and the cruelty of the natural world. His work epitomized the view that value resided in the designer's vision and the craftsman's skill rather than the size and quality of the gemstones, and many of his pieces are made chiefly of non-precious materials such as horn and glass. Botanical imagery changed radically in his hands from static flower-heads of densely-packed diamonds to flowing, fragile confections of enamelled gold, coloured stones, opalescent glass and horn. These were combined with an exceptional understanding of colour and texture, along with a close observation of nature which endowed his work with a feeling for the spirit of the subject beyond its physical reality. Insects were another major source of inspiration, with fragile damselflies and 129 wasps in enamelled gold, and necklaces of horn grasshoppers. Gradually his interest in glass – which had been a major component of some of his

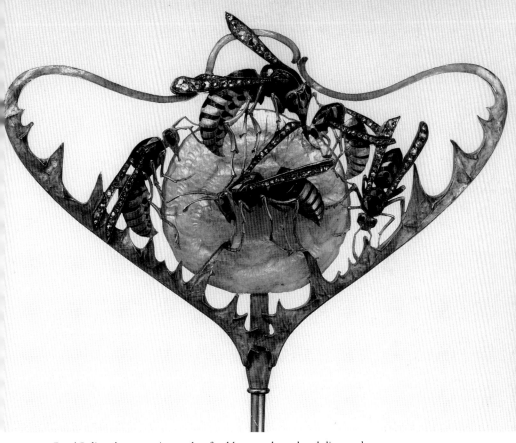

129 René Lalique's wasps pin, made of gold, enamel, opal and diamonds, was shown at the Paris Exhibition of 1900. The artistic and technical excellence that characterize Lalique's work transform a subject that might conventionally seem repellent into one of fascination.

finest pieces – overshadowed his work as a jeweller. In 1910 he purchased a glass-works and abandoned goldsmiths' work almost entirely (see below, p. 182).

Art nouveau jewelry often features highly sophisticated enamel work. Most impressive is *plique-à-jour*, a difficult technique that creates a delicate stained-glass effect without a metal backplate. One of its most successful practitioners was Eugène Feuillâtre (1870–1916), who had formerly worked for Lalique before establishing his own business in 1897. In Brussels Philippe Wolfers (1858–1929) achieved similarly high standards in the series of Art Nouveau jewels he created around the turn of the century.

137

137

130 Lucien Gaillard was a master in the creation of decorative horn combs such as this one, of *c.* 1900–1905, with a cresting of Japanese quince blossom. Made of partly tinted horn and diamonds, it is a substantial piece, 14.7 cm (nearly 6 in.) wide.

Another distinctive material, horn, was bleached to the colour of pale honey and carved into various ornaments, but chiefly elaborate combs decorated with flowers, sycamore seeds and butterflies. Lucien Gaillard (1861-1933), who employed Japanese craftsmen, made many of the 130 finest, with tinted petals and diamond-tipped stamens.

Amongst Lalique's contemporaries, Maison Vever were particularly distinguished. Also winners of a prestigious *Grand Prix* in 1900, they differed in their use of high quality precious stones and their adherence to conventional gem-setting techniques, sympathetically adapting them to the new forms of Art Nouveau. Under the creative direction of Henri Vever (1854–1942) magnificent botanical designs were created in close-ly-set diamonds. Figurative enamelled jewels were also made, some 131 designed by the artist Eugène Grasset (1845–1917). Henri Vever's schol-arly study *La Bijouterie française au XIXe siècle* remains an invaluable source of information on 19th-century French jewelry.

Georges Fouquet (1862–1957) took over his father's well-established firm in 1895. The Czech painter Alphonse Mucha (1860–1939) created a striking new Art Nouveau shop for him and also designed some 132 jewelry, notably a serpent bracelet and ring linked by jewelled chains

131 Diamond-encrusted fern tiara, shown by Henri Vever at the Paris Exhibition of 1900. The asymmetrical entwined fronds exemplify the flowing lines of Art Nouveau.

132 The jeweller Georges Fouquet and the artist Alphonse Mucha worked together to produce this serpent bracelet and connected ring for Sarah Bernhardt in 1899. The materials are gold, diamonds, rubies and a mosaic of opals.

132   for the actress Sarah Bernhardt in 1899. Most of the design work between 1899 and 1914 was done by Charles Desrosiers, who specialized in graceful floral motifs, although he also depicted the sinuous imaginary monsters typical of Art Nouveau. Fouquet's enamellers, particularly Etienne Tourette, reached new heights of virtuosity in *plique-à-jour* by incorporating tiny flakes of gold or silver foil to produce a shimmering effect.

Manufacturing jewellers from all over the world visited the Paris Exhibition. Firms such as Unger Brothers and William Kerr of Newark, New Jersey, began mass-producing Art Nouveau pieces in silver sheet after 1900. The same happened in the important costume jewelry city of Gablonz in Bohemia (now Jablonec in the Czech Republic). In Paris inexpensive, good quality Art Nouveau jewelry was made by Piel Frères. 'Artistic' jewelry became much more widely available, but popularization in turn contributed to the decline of the style, as the leading designers looked for new forms of expression.

In Britain the Pre-Raphaelites with their notions of aesthetic dress and artistic jewelry had begun to influence fashion by the late 1870s, and their appreciation of unusual materials and hand-crafted work formed a direct link with the Arts and Crafts jewellers of the next generation. The Arts and Crafts movement was dedicated not only to reform in design, but also to the dignity of the individual craftsman as expounded by William Morris and John Ruskin in reaction to mechanization and mass-production. It encompassed a variety of individual styles, but distinctive characteristics include hand-beaten metal surfaces, soft-coloured cabochon stones, enamel-work, and a preference for decorative themes from a romanticized pre-industrial past. At its centre were the Art Workers Guild, and the Arts and Crafts Exhibition Society through which work was shown and sold. Members included amateurs as well as skilled jewellers, and some of the most interesting pieces were designed by architects such as C. R. Ashbee (1863–1942), Henry Wilson (1864–1934) and John Paul Cooper (1869–1933). The sculptor Sir Alfred Gilbert (1854–1934) made innovative jewelry from loosely tangled silver wire set with glass stones. 139, 133 140

One of the guilds which followed Ruskin's theories most rigorously, and which was to have a great influence in England and the Continent, was the Guild of Handicraft, established by Ashbee in 1888. It was based initially in the East End of London, where young men, untouched by commercial practices or formal training, were taught metalworking by Ashbee from his own translation of Cellini's notebooks. At first they made simple silver brooches and clasps, often incorporating curving wire decoration and panels of plain-coloured enamel. As their skills increased, they produced more complex pieces in enamelled gold set with mother-of-pearl and gemstones. These more elaborate jewels, often versions of Ashbee's favourite motifs of a peacock or a sailing boat, were neatly finished but often assembled using rather unconventional methods. In 1902 the Guild moved to Chipping Camden in Gloucestershire and in 1908 it closed down. Its influence on English jewelry can be seen in Liberty's success at selling stylistically similar machine-produced pieces, while its international significance was recognized when Josef Hoffmann in Vienna took it as a model for the Wiener Werkstätte. 139

The work of Henry Wilson, who began making jewelry in the 1890s, is characterized by a richness of colour and form, with brilliant enamels and soft cabochon stones set into elaborately modelled settings. He had been briefly in partnership with the influential enameller Alexander 133

133 Tiara by Henry Wilson of enamelled gold set with rock crystal, moonstones, pearls, star sapphires and rubies, *c.* 1909. The fitting at the back was designed to hold the ostrich feathers required for presentation at court. It is a rare example of so formal a piece in the English Arts and Crafts style.

140 Fisher (1864–1936) who, through his teaching and his articles in the *Studio* magazine, had done much to revive painted enamels. It was at Wilson's studio that John Paul Cooper trained, and this connection is apparent in the style and colouring of much of his work, although he often added a distinctive gold border of foliage and flowers. Both Wilson and Cooper were effective teachers, passing on the craft ethos to succeeding generations of students.

140 Also known for their enamelled jewelry were Nelson and Edith Dawson (1864–1939 and 1862–1928) who founded the Artificers' Guild in 1901. Nelson had learnt enamelling from Fisher, but it was his wife Edith, taught by him, who painted their distinctive richly-coloured enamel plaques, usually of flowers or insects. Another important husband-and-wife team, Arthur and Georgie Cave Gaskin (1862–1928 and 1868–1934), was based in Birmingham. They worked together from 1899, Georgie doing most of the design work, Arthur doing the enamelling, the rest of the work being shared between them and their assistants. Their delicate necklaces, densely patterned with small leaves, flowers and birds, remained in production until the 1920s.

The Scottish Arts and Crafts movement developed slightly differently from its English counterpart, more closely affected by Art Nouveau and

166

the Symbolist painters of Continental Europe. The Edinburgh artist-craftswoman Phoebe Traquair (1852–1936) painted mermaids, cupids and 140 angels in translucent enamel, with gold or silver foils set between the layers. In Aberdeen James Cromar Watt (1862–1940) used the same technique to produce more abstract naturalistic patterns. A distinctive style emerged in Glasgow around the School of Art and the circle of Charles Rennie Mackintosh (1868–1928). He left only one or two drawings for jewelry, but pieces survive by – among others – Peter Wylie Davidson, who taught at the School; and Jessie M. King (1876-1949) provided designs for Liberty's in London.

Liberty's did much to popularize the Arts and Crafts style, primarily through the 'Cymric' range which was launched in 1899. This was an 134 extremely successful venture, both artistically and financially: designers of outstanding skill were employed – though their names were almost never divulged at the time – and Liberty's acceptance of machine production (by Haselers of Birmingham) enabled them to undercut the prices of craftsmen committed to working only by hand. Although some more lavish pieces in gold were really made by hand, in the more common

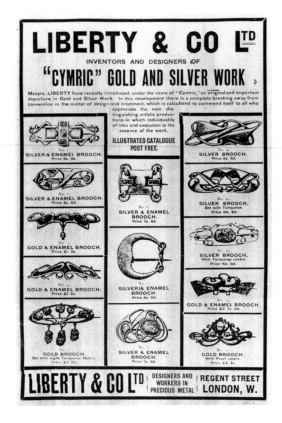

134 Advertisement of 1902 for Liberty's 'Cymric' brooches. Machine-produced but designed to look hand-made, they diffused Arts and Crafts forms to a wide clientele. Prices started at less than 6 shillings.

silver work mass-production was cleverly disguised, for instance by incorporating mock hammer-marks into the stamping dies. Celtic interlace and stylized botanical motifs were the most common patterns, usually in sinuous silver openwork decorated with enamels. Turquoises, opals, moonstones and blister pearls were sometimes used, even though they required setting by hand. A simple technique, whereby they were set behind a hole in the silver rather than within a separate collet, created an elegant effect with the stone appearing to grow out of the metal.

Archibald Knox (1864–1933) contributed the largest number of designs for the Cymric scheme during its finest years from 1899 to 1912. His subtle and elegant adaptation of Celtic interlace (as a Manxman he was himself a Celt) is one of the most distinctive features of Liberty's jewelry from this period, and his ability to make the patterns suitable for machine production showed impressive technical skill. Other principal designers were Jessie M. King and Rex Silver (1879–1965) of the Silver Studio.

135, 138 The Wiener Werkstätte (literally, Vienna Workshops) were responsible for the most innovatory jewelry produced in Austria in the early 20th century, with its graceful outlines related to French Art Nouveau, yet tempered by the work of the Austrian Secession movement and the stirrings of Modernism. They were founded in 1903 by Josef Hoffmann (1870–1956) and Koloman Moser (1868–1918), and financed by the banker Fritz Wärndorfer, with the aim of improving every aspect of contemporary design. Like Ashbee's Guild of Handicraft the Werkstätte preferred to use colourful semi-precious stones, and pieces were made by

135 Brooch by the architect and designer Josef Hoffmann, co-founder of the Wiener Werkstätte. Of silver set with malachite and moss agate, it dates from c. 1910–11.

136 opposite 'Ice' pendant, of rock crystal set with diamonds in platinum. This piece was bought from Fabergé's London shop on 23 December 1913 for £60.

168

137 *above* Much of the subtlety of colouring in Art Nouveau jewelry was achieved with enamel. Here it is the difficult technique of translucent *plique-à-jour:* (top) pendant of a woman in woodland, set with diamonds and a peridot, bearing the mark of José Descomps, French, *c.* 1900; (left) orchid hair ornament by Philippe Wolfers, set with rubies and diamonds, 1902; (below) peacock pendant set with diamonds, opals and emeralds, bearing the mark of L. Gautrait, Paris, *c.* 1900.

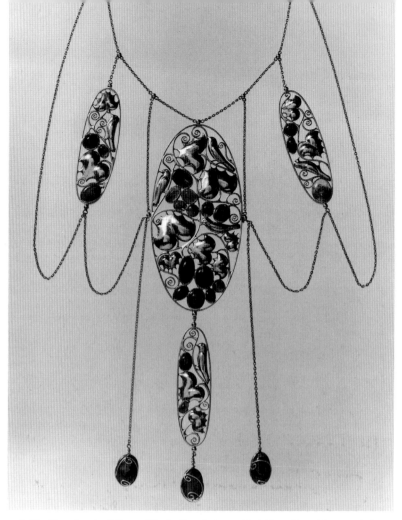

138 Necklace by the Wiener Werkstätte designer Carl Otto Czeschka, consisting of four oval pendants filled with a web-like pattern of birds and foliage in gold and opals connected by a series of looped chains, *c.* 1905.

hand, but they employed fully trained craftsmen, and so achieved a more
135 professional result. Hoffmann and Moser created rather minimalist linear patterns, based on simple geometric forms or stylized foliage. In 1905
138 Carl Otto Czeschka (1878–1960) became involved, designing more florid and densely ornamented jewelry, a trend further advanced with the arrival of Dagobert Peche (1887–1923) in 1915. Around this time carved ivory plaques were introduced, set as brooches or in a necklace. Peche's

170

fanciful and exuberant approach was in marked contrast to the restraint of the founding designers, but it was to become the group's dominant style into the 1920s. By 1926 financial problems forced the Wiener Werkstätte into receivership, and they closed down finally in 1932.

In Germany the craft ideal and Art Nouveau were being explored at the turn of the century by individual workshops in Munich, Darmstadt, Weimar and Berlin. Best known of these was the artists' colony at Darmstadt, founded in 1899 by Grand Duke Ernst Ludwig of Hessen, which offered purpose-built houses and workshops for artists and crafts-men and their families. Among those who designed jewelry were the architects Peter Behrens (1869–1940) and Josef Olbrich (1867–1908); some, like Patriz Huber (1878–1902), worked not only for one-off craft manufacture but also for mass-production by the important Pforzheim manufacturer Theodor Fahrner. At Weimar the head of the Art School, the Belgian architect Henry van de Velde (1863–1957), produced jewelry designs with flowing linear motifs typical of Art Nouveau.

Danish design rose to prominence in the early years of the 20th century with a style that was clearly related to developments in the rest of Europe but distinctively Scandinavian. Recent trends in England and France had been seen in Copenhagen through an exhibition of Ashbee's work in 1899, and then through the new Danish Museum of Decorative Art's acquisition of work by Lalique and other Art Nouveau jewellers in 1900. The new Danish style, known as *skønvirke* or 'aesthetic work', was pioneered by a small group of artists, architects and craftsmen, who achieved effects of extraordinary plasticity and created a highly distinc-tive look characterized by abstract, rounded forms. Silver was the preferred material, worked in high relief and left with a surface pattern-ing of hammer marks. Enamel was almost never used: instead, semi-precious cabochons served to add colour.

The earliest *skønvirke* designs, of the late 1890s, were by the architect Thorvald Bindesbøll (1846–1908). Conventional workshops found them difficult to produce, as the fluid forms were so different from the jewelry they were used to making, but from 1904 he worked very successfully with the silversmith Holger Kyster (1872–1944). The artist Mogens Ballin (1871–1914) established his workshop in 1900, and produced jewelry with powerfully organic fluid forms in silver, copper, brass and pewter set with semi-precious stones such as lapis lazuli, amethyst, amber and agate. Most of the design work was done by Ballin himself or by the sculptor Siegfried Wagner (1874–1952). Georg Jensen (1866–1935), 142 the most famous of Danish jewellers, trained as a goldsmith and a sculptor before spending two formative years with Ballin. He established

139 *opposite, above* Jewelry designed by C. R. Ashbee and made by the Guild of Handicraft: (left) brooch of enamelled copper, silver wire and blister pearls, *c.* 1896; (centre) necklace with peacock pendant, of silver, gold, blister pearls, diamond sparks and a demantoid garnet for the eye, 1991; (right) ship pendant of enamelled gold, opal, diamond sparks and tourmalines, *c.* 1903.

140 *opposite, below* Arts and Crafts jewelry: (top) necklace in silver, gold, opals and topaz made by the Gaskins in the style they developed *c.* 1910; (centre) necklace with painted enamel plaques by Phoebe Traquair, *c.* 1905; (centre, below) pendant of enamelled gold irises with opal and amethyst drops by the Dawsons, 1900; (below left) silver wire jewelry set with pastes made by the sculptor Alfred Gilbert; (below right) pendant by Alexander Fisher, of steel with a painted enamel plaque, *c.* 1895.

141 *above* 'Peacock' necklace by Louis Comfort Tiffany of New York, of gold, a mosaic of opals, and amethysts, sapphires, demantoid garnets, rubies and emeralds, *c.* 1905.

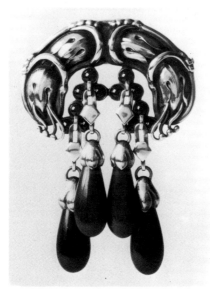

142 Brooch in hand-beaten silver
and semi-precious stones, designed
by Georg Jensen of Copenhagen
in 1906.

142 his own workshop in 1904, and international acclaim soon followed.
While Jensen designed many of the pieces himself, he also employed
skilled draughtsmen and artists to work in a similar idiom, and their contribution was always acknowledged by the firm. One of the most prolific
of Danish jewellers in the *skønvirke* style was Evald Nielsen (1879–1958),
who had his own workshop from 1907.

141 American Arts and Crafts and Art Nouveau flourished in parallel with
their European counterparts. The finest jewelry was made by Louis
Comfort Tiffany (1848–1933) – the son of the founder of Tiffany & Co.
– who is better known for his iridescent Favrile glass and vibrant
stained-glass windows. From around 1902 to 1907 he employed his own
craftsmen at Tiffany Furnaces; fine enamels were made by Julia Munson,
while his renowned glass-makers contributed strings of magnificently
coloured lustrous beads. His jewelry, of gold rather than silver, combined
the deliberate irregularity of hand-wrought Arts and Crafts metal with
vivid enamel-work and richly coloured gemstones, producing an effect
of exotic opulence. In general early pieces are characterized by a rich
naturalism and very vivid colours, whereas later ones tend to be more
restrained and symmetrical. From 1907 his designs were made in the
workshops of Tiffany & Co. and sold through the newly established
'Art Jewelry' department in their New York building.

CHAPTER EIGHT

From Art Deco to the 1950s

The linear forms characteristic of the Art Deco style began to emerge in jewelry as early as 1910, but it was in the years between the First and Second World Wars that the style was at its height. The end of the First World War in 1918 had allowed a return to extravagance among the wealthy, but the mood of society had changed, and now stylized and geometric motifs emerged. High-value faceted gemstones returned in profusion as a major element of jewelry, and together with the vibrant colour contrasts of semi-precious materials like turquoise and coral created exotic effects far removed from the subtly shaded enamels of the preceding decades. The stark, original style was eventually named 'Art Deco', after the Paris Exposition Internationale des Arts Décoratifs et Industriels Modernes of 1925.

Many influences contributed to Art Deco, including the geometry and abstraction of the Cubist painters and the linear forms of the Vienna Secession. Diaghilev's Ballets Russes, performing in Paris from 1909, encouraged exotic and dramatic combinations of colour. The discovery of Tutankhamun's tomb in 1922 inspired the use of Egyptian themes, and motifs were also borrowed from India and the Far East. Technology had a powerful influence, with simple angular and cylindrical shapes combined, often overlapping or assembled in a way that resembled parts of a machine. Bold forms, polished surfaces and blocks of gemstones replaced subtle detailing and, in keeping with a 'functional' approach, surface decoration was minimal.

The established Parisian jewelry dynasties were at the forefront of the new style, and as some of them now had branches in London and New York they exerted a direct influence on an international level. The style required two skills at which they excelled – careful matching of stones and impeccable stone-setting techniques – and the quality of work in the finest gem-set pieces was exceptionally high. The basic forms developed from pre-war models which had already shown how best to complement the straighter, looser, and now shorter fashions. The emphasis remained on elegant vertical lines: necklaces hung low, often with an elaborate jewelled pendant, while long earrings accompanied the new short hairstyles.

144 *left* Cartier's panther jewelry, dating back to a geometric piece of 1915 with a surface pattern of diamonds and black onyx spots, developed into a zoomorphic form of lasting popularity. The range was supervised by Jeanne Toussaint, whose nickname was 'Panthère'. In this clip made for the Duchess of Windsor in 1949 the panther, pavé-set with diamonds and sapphires, with yellow diamond eyes, is elegantly balanced on a large cabochon sapphire.

145 *below* In England the craft tradition remained strong. Sybil Dunlop is notable for her subtle combinations of colourful stones: this brooch, of silver set with opal, tourmaline, moonstone, sapphire, citrine and amethyst, dates from *c.* 1925.

143 *opposite* Bodice ornament designed by Lucien Hirtz for the 1925 Exposition des Arts Décoratifs in Paris. It is made as a mosaic of lapis-lazuli, jade, coral and onyx; where the original was edged with diamonds, this version is set with paste. The turquoise drop and silken tassel are later reconstructions.

Sleeveless dresses and the shedding of evening gloves encouraged the wearing of bracelets, especially gem-encrusted geometric link types which were to remain in fashion until the outbreak of the Second World War. Brooches tended to be small, and were worn on the shoulder or pinned to a belt or hat. The most characteristic brooch design consists of a central ring of onyx or crystal decorated with a diamond-set lozenge or bar at each side; others were in the form of stylized trees and baskets of colourful flowers. Black and white became a very fashionable combination in the mid-1920s, and black onyx – coloured by soaking agate in sugar solution then heating it in sulphuric acid – was in great demand. At the same time materials of strongly contrasting colours such as jade, coral, turquoise and lapis lazuli were frequently used together. 146 146 143

Rings in the the 1920s might be set with a large cabochon stone, often surrounded by small brilliants or by the recently introduced rectangular baguette diamonds. Platinum was chosen for wedding rings, frequently worn with a platinum and diamond solitaire engagement ring. An alternative was Cartier's 'Trinity' ring made of three interlocking hoops of polished red, yellow and white gold, which was introduced in 1924. Solitaires set with rectangular emerald-cut diamonds were typical in the years around 1925.

Some of the finest pieces from the 1920s were made by Cartier, who combined superb stones with excellent design and the most stringent quality control. By this date, the three Cartier brothers – Louis (1875–1942), Pierre (1878–1965) and Jacques (1884–1942) – were running branches in Paris, New York and London respectively; and Jeanne Toussaint (1887–1978), who was responsible for many of Cartier's most successful designs until the late 1950s, was working for them in Paris. They and the other fashionable firms of the Rue de la Paix and the Place Vendôme, such as Boucheron, Mauboussin and Van Cleef & Arpels, pioneered an exotic cosmopolitan approach. 144

In imitation of Indian Moghul jewelry, irregular polished or ribbed emerald beads were strung as necklaces, often with a large pendant of carved emerald or rock crystal framed with diamonds. Emeralds, sapphires and rubies were carved into leaves and flowers and assembled as brooches, or, inspired by the Indian 'Tree of Life', densely packed along a diamond branch to make a bracelet or necklace. In the mid-1920s jewellers began also to use Chinese motifs. Here too, original jade carvings were often incorporated, usually framed with delicate borders of diamonds and geometric bands of black onyx, or mounted as drops on long pendant earrings. Sharply in contrast to these intricate pieces was the craze for 148 146

146 Art Deco diamond jewelry before 1930: (left) pendant brooch in the form of an ornamental tree made of carved gems, in a diamond frame in the Chinese style, French, c. 1925; (above right) early lozenge-shaped brooch of diamonds and black onyx set in platinum, made in Paris c. 1912; (below right) cypress tree brooch, of diamonds, black onyx and emeralds set in platinum and white gold, c. 1927.

147 Diamond brooches of 1930–40: (above left) brooch with gems carved to resemble
flowers and a long loop of baguette-cut diamonds tipped with two sapphire drops,
French, *c.* 1930; (above right) brooch of brilliant and baguette-cut diamonds and cabochon
emeralds, which can be adapted to make a flexible pendant, French, *c.* 1930–40; (centre)
brooch in the form of a tree with diamonds, rubies, emeralds and sapphires, French,
bearing the mark Ostertag, *c.* 1930–40; (below left) double clip of brilliant, baguette and
square-cut diamonds which divides into two matching brooches, *c.* 1930–40; (below
right) brilliant and baguette-cut diamond clip by Cartier of London, *c.* 1940.

148 Necklace and earrings of carved emeralds, sapphires and rubies, with brilliant-cut diamonds. The design, based on the popular 'Tree of Life' motif from India, was created by Cartier in 1936 for the American socialite Daisy Fellowes.

African jewelry – particularly bangles of ivory or glazed wood – encouraged by Josephine Baker's *Revue nègre* and the Colonial Exhibitions held in Marseilles in 1922 and Paris in 1931.

Designs in precious materials were imitated by the firms making costume jewelry. Theodor Fahrner of Pforzheim in Germany produced stylish geometric pieces in which panels of marcasite are interspersed with blocks of coloured semi-precious stones or glass. Bakelite, a plastic patented in 1907, was used to make bright beads and bangles, and combined with chromium-plated elements to make necklaces. Throughout the 1920s and 1930s Henkel & Grosse of Pforzheim made jewelry of Bakelite and a white base-metal alloy they patented as 'platinin'. In France one of the foremost companies in this field was Maison Auguste Bonaz, based in Oyonnax near the Swiss border. Manufacturers in the region had previously made decorative combs, but with the cropped hair of the 1920s they turned instead to jewelry in brightly coloured celluloid.

High quality mass-produced glass jewelry was designed during the 1920s by Lalique. Brightly coloured rings were cast in one piece, while necklaces and bracelets were made from intricately moulded identical beads. For brooches and cufflinks moulded glass panels were mounted in plain gold frames, perhaps with a tinted foil behind to enhance the colour. Much of the naturalistic imagery Lalique had used in his Art Nouveau jewelry reappeared in this later work, but alongside were abstract Art Deco forms. An alternative material called *pâte de verre* was used by Lalique's contemporary, Gabriel Argy-Rousseau (1860–1945). Made from a paste of finely ground glass coloured with metal oxides, it could be sculpted or pressed into shape while cold, before being fired and then cooled very slowly. It was an arduous process but allowed more variety than moulded glass. It was principally used for circular floral pendants which were worn on long silk cords, usually with silk tassels hanging below.

A much starker and flatter geometric style of jewelry, dominated by the forms of technology and engineering, was the main alternative to the colourful exotic pieces described above. In simple interlocking or layered shapes, flat surfaces of platinum, gold, silver or steel were placed alongside panels of coloured hardstone or enamel, often with a discreet line of diamonds in between or with a large coloured stone such as aquamarine or topaz at the centre. Surface decoration was minimal, and the functionalism of the designs was reinforced by the use of forms resembling machine parts. The most substantial and powerful pieces originated from a small nucleus of avant-garde artists and jewellers in Paris in the 1920s, at the centre of which were Raymond Templier (1891–1968) and Jean Fouquet (1899–1984), both of whom had been born into important

149

149 Jean Fouquet was one of the most influential jewellers working in the stark, mechanistic style that emerged in Paris in the 1920s. In this pendant that he designed in 1929, a flat, polished slab of platinum is contrasted with two vertical bands of diamonds and a central cabochon sapphire.

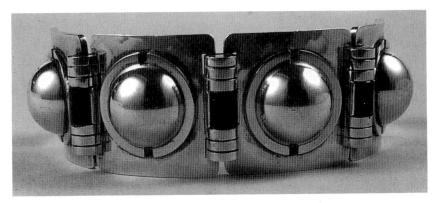

150 Bracelet by Jean Desprès, of silver and silver-gilt with bars of black onyx set into the hinges, 1930. The metal elements of the hinges are reminiscent of the forms of machinery.

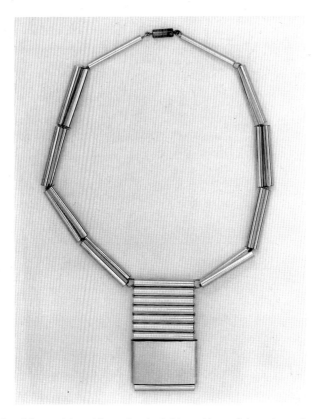

152 Industrial materials and forms inspired this necklace of chromium-plated brass tubes by the Bauhaus designer Naum Slutzky. Designed in 1929 when the Bauhaus was in Dessau, the piece was re-made by Slutzky in 1960.

families of jewellers, and Jean Desprès (1889–1980), whose training had been in industrial design.   150

In Germany, similarly radical approaches were being explored by students and teachers at the Bauhaus, the influential school founded by Walter Gropius in Weimar in 1919, which sought to apply the imagery of industry and technology to design in all areas. Bauhaus theories were explored in jewelry by Naum Slutzky (1894–1965), who worked mainly   152 in chromium-plated brass or silver to produce stark geometric forms which sometimes incorporated a single colour of enamel, or a panel of wood, haematite or quartz. Precious metals were difficult to obtain in Germany during the Depression of the 1920s, but these unconventional

151 Ruby and diamond brooch by Van Cleef & Arpels, given by Edward VIII to Mrs Simpson at Christmas 1936. The rubies are *calibré*-cut and invisibly set, a technique developed by Van Cleef & Arpels in 1935, while the diamonds are conventionally set in platinum. The earrings are in the same style but later.

and inexpensive materials were perhaps better suited to Slutzky's uncompromising and austere work. When the Bauhaus was closed by the Nazis in 1933 many of its teachers and students fled abroad, greatly influencing the development of the modern jewelry movement. László Moholy-Nagy (1895–1946), who had been in charge of the metal workshop, moved to Chicago where his pupils included Margaret de Patta (see p. 193). Slutzky was foremost among those who came to England, where he taught metalwork and industrial design.

In Britain, although Art Deco became the dominant style the Arts and Crafts tradition was sustained well into the 1930s by a second generation of jewellers. They included H. G. Murphy (1884–1939), a pupil of Henry Wilson and admirer of the Ballets Russes, and Sybil Dunlop (1889–1968), who had trained in Brussels. Both used concentrations of unusual and variously coloured stones to create pattern. In the 1930s the Birmingham jeweller George Hunt (1892–1960) combined his Arts and Crafts style with such fashionable themes as the art of Egypt and the Far East, in pieces similarly characterized by unusual materials and bright colours. In Australia too the Arts and Crafts movement continued to flourish, with a committed circle of craftsmen amongst whom the best-known and most prolific was Rhoda Wager (1875–1953) of Sydney. Between the early 1920s and the mid-1940s she produced thousands of pieces, often drawing on distinctively Australian themes and materials, and all carefully recorded in her sketchbooks.

Accessories became an essential part of women's jewelry, particularly decorated frames for evening bags, cigarette holders and powder compacts. Smoking and the wearing of cosmetics had only recently become acceptable in polite society, and the slight element of daring they retained ensured that both became fashionable. The geometric style of Art Deco was well suited to such functional items, and sleek boxes and vanity cases were made in enamelled or lacquered gold, sometimes with decorative panels of carved hardstones and outlines drawn in rows of tiny brilliant-cut diamonds. Less costly versions favoured such unusual materials as shagreen (the granular skin of the ray or shark which was polished and stained) and *coquille d'oeuf* (a mosaic of crushed eggshell). In the early 1930s a new style of vanity case called a *minaudière* was designed by Van Cleef & Arpels. This complex box contained compartments which were specially designed for essentials such as lipstick, powder, rouge, a watch, cigarettes and lighter.

Fine jewelry of the early 1930s was often 'all-white', made solely of diamonds set in platinum or white gold. As in the 1920s the stones covered the surface, and pattern and variety were achieved through

145

147

different shapes and cuts. Round brilliant-cut and rectangular baguette-cut diamonds were most commonly used, with ovals, pointed marquises and briolette drops interspersed. Patterns were becoming less angular, with shapes softening into curves, loops, spirals and continuous motifs such as link and ribbon interlace. Within the heavier three-dimensional forms of the later 1930s rounded pleats and ruff motifs are formed in the diamond-encrusted metal.

Elegant diamond jewelry continued to be worn in Europe until the outbreak of the Second World War: tiaras remained an integral part of English court jewelry, and new flatter styles which framed the face were introduced during the 1930s. Earrings were long, and necklaces typically consisted of substantial square-linked diamond-encrusted chains. Polychrome jewelry made of carved Indian stones remained popular, with Cartier making a particularly fine necklace in this style for the American 148 socialite Daisy Fellowes in 1936. For less formal occasions, the most distinctive and versatile item of jewelry in the 1930s was the double clip, 147 which could be worn as a single large piece or as a smaller matching pair of brooches. Rings were complex and large, their bezels encrusted with stones of different colours and cuts arranged in compact geometric patterns. Their chunky angular forms gradually softened into more rounded volutes, barrels, fans and turbans.

The shape of earrings underwent a radical change due to the widespread adoption of the new clip fitting: they became more compact, and the decoration was concentrated around the lobe, sometimes even extending upwards following the curve of the ear. Popular styles included scrolls and spirals, and increasingly naturalistic images such as flower-heads, curled leaves and cornucopias.

An ingenious innovation in gem-set jewelry was introduced in 1935 by Van Cleef & Arpels, who developed invisible settings that could be used to create mosaic-like surfaces of precious stones. It was an intricate technique requiring lapidaries of the highest skill. Rubies and sapphires were most often used, mounted so as to give uninterrupted panels of either red or blue. They were *calibré*-cut – each one individually shaped according to its exact place in the design – and held edge to edge invisibly by fine metal rods beneath the surface. One of the earliest and most striking jewels made in this way is a brooch given by Edward VIII 151 in 1936 to Mrs Simpson, who after his abdication became his wife and Duchess of Windsor. The technique was immediately adopted by other makers and was frequently imitated in costume jewelry.

Costume jewelry reached new artistic heights in Paris in the late 1920s and 1930s, with influential couturiers, notably Coco Chanel (1883–1971) and Elsa Schiaparelli (1890–1973), encouraging their wealthy clients to wear extravagant and theatrical '*bijoux de fantaisie*'. They were catering not for those who aspired to wealth but for those who already owned genuine jewels, and this gave them greater freedom to create imaginative and exciting pieces. Chanel challenged conventions by mixing genuine and fake, and evening jewelry with daytime clothes. She often used imitation pearls, usually large baroque ones, strung with a variety of coloured glass stones. Many of her finest pieces from the mid-1920s to 1934 were designed by Fulco Santostefano della Cerda, Duke of Verdura (1895–1978), whose privileged and eccentric life in Sicily (which had culminated with his spending the last of his inheritance on a fancy dress ball) provided a wonderful source of inspiration. Schiaparelli's jewelry was of a more unusual, even bizarre, character, particularly those pieces designed by her Surrealist friends, such as electrically-lit jewelry by Jean Clément and a necklace of aspirins by the poet Louis Aragon. From the late 1930s until the outbreak of war her principal designer was Jean Schlumberger (1907–87). From the late 1940s Line Vautrin developed an exclusive following for her quirky and witty costume jewelry made of gilded bronze.

Although platinum settings remained typical for evening wear, there was a dramatic change in the appearance of less formal jewelry in the second half of the 1930s, with the reintroduction of yellow gold. Flexible
154 tube necklaces were made from closely interlocking identical links, and often worn with a decorative pendant. They were known as 'gas-pipes' or 'serpents' and remained fashionable until at least the end of the 1940s. Chunky articulated bracelets with repeating angular or soft pleated forms were also made in gold.

Between 1939 and 1945 the Second World War brought a large part of the jewelry industry in Europe to a halt. In addition to the conscription of craftsmen and the bombing of manufacturing centres, materials were scarce due to the disruption of the gem trade and restrictions on the use of precious metals (platinum, for instance, was required by the armaments industry, further promoting the use of gold), and additional taxes were imposed on jewelry. Re-setting and new work did continue, however, as can be seen in the design albums of some of the major firms. During the
153 war Cartier made brooches depicting a caged bird, symbolizing the Nazi occupation of Paris, and celebrated the Liberation in 1944 with the same metaphor but with the cage door open and the bird in song.

Naturalistic motifs predominated, characterized by asymmetry and a feeling of spontaneity and movement. Brooches appeared in the form
154 of exotic birds and animals, and bouquets of flowers (this time with stems

188

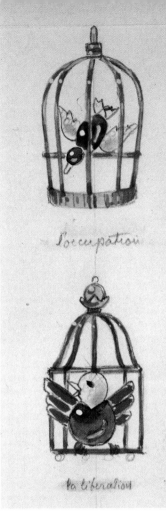

153 Brooch designs by Cartier symbolizing the wartime plight of Paris: the caged bird at the top is marked 'l'occupation – juin 1940', while in the design below, 'la libération – août 1944', the cage is open and the bird is in song.

of polished gold and each petal made from a single large coloured stone). The informal and lighthearted treatment of conventional subjects continued into the 1950s. Less valuable stones such as aquamarines, citrines and amethysts were used in large quantities to make extravagant multi-coloured pieces, and gold surfaces were polished to a high shine or textured with a woven or twisted-rope pattern. By the 1950s platinum was available again, and the similar but slightly lighter palladium was introduced. Necklaces were large, designed to complement the low necklines, narrow waists and full skirts of the 'New Look' launched by Dior in 1947. Bib necklaces, which are deeper at the front, were

155

155

154 Jewelry of 1939–40, of gold and bright-coloured gems. The 'gas-pipe' or 'serpent' necklace has floral *passe-partout* clips attached, of yellow and blue sapphires and rubies. The 'Grand Bouquet' lapel brooch combines polished gold stems and leaves with blue sapphire and ruby flowers. All are by Van Cleef & Arpels.

introduced around this time. Earclips remained the standard type of earring, but they often now came with cascades of stones or finely woven gold tassels which could be attached for evening wear.

The American jewelry industry had been far less affected than its European counterparts by the war, and encouraged by a very wealthy clientele had evolved with increased stylistic independence. There was a greater emphasis on gems, often with unusual geometric cuts, arranged in random clusters and held in place by large claws. The most famous of those working with large precious stones was Harry Winston (1896–

155 An angular bib necklace of twisted gold rope set with amethysts, turquoises and diamonds, made by Cartier for the Duchess of Windsor in 1947.

1978) in New York. He specialized in important diamonds, and his interest was in their size and quality rather than the design of the setting, which was kept very simple. Paul Flato created bold and heavy pieces for many of the Hollywood stars from the 1930s, with diamond solitaires so angular and large that they were known as 'ice-cubes'. His most characteristic jewelry consists of chunky, plain gold letters linked together to spell out initials, names or sentiments.

Verdura worked briefly for Flato before establishing his own firm in New York in 1939. There until the 1960s he created witty and whimsical jewels in richly coloured semi-precious stones and oddly shaped baroque pearls. One of the earliest themes he explored after opening his own shop was that of decorating real seashells with gold and gems, an idea much imitated by other jewellers in America during the 1950s. Unusual botanical subjects were also a regular feature of his work. Another émigré, Jean Schlumberger, worked in a similarly colourful sculptural style. His New York shop opened in 1946, selling distinctive jewels shaped as starfish, sea horses, flowers and birds. In 1956 he joined Tiffany as senior designer, combining his flamboyant interpretation of nature with magnificent gemstones.

High quality costume jewelry flourished in America where it was centred in Providence, Rhode Island. Among the most successful firms was Eisenberg, who had begun as garment manufacturers giving away a free brooch with every coat; another, Trifari, from 1930 benefited from the skills of the French designer Alfred Philippe, who had worked in precious metals for Van Cleef & Arpels. Joseff of Hollywood, known as 'Jeweller to the Stars', established himself as a designer for films before launching his retail range of 'movie-star jewelry' in 1938. One of the most influential of the American costume jewellers of the 1940s and 1950s was Miriam Haskell, whose work, typically imitating tiny seed pearls and gold filigree, was inspired by Byzantine and Indian models.

Most of the significant jewelry made in Europe and America from the 1920s to the 1950s had used precious metals and fine gemstones, and had

156 After designing costume jewelry for Chanel in Paris, Verdura emigrated to America where he realized similarly whimsical designs in real stones. This pomegranate brooch of faceted peridots and cabochon rubies set in gold dates from the late 1930s when he was working for Paul Flato.

157 Echoing the spirit of his larger work, the sculptor Alexander Calder made distinctive jewelry from the 1930s onwards, mostly for his friends and family. This necklace of coiled brass wire dates from *c.* 1938.

required the most exacting levels of craftsmanship. Towards the end of the period, however, some notable alternative or artistic designers emerged, among them the American sculptor Alexander Calder (1898–1976), best known for his mobiles with finely balanced moving parts. His jewelry usually consists of repeated forms made in thick copper or brass wire. He uses strong and simple forms such as spirals, and references to primitive civilizations implicit in these shapes are emphasized by the use of this ancient technique. More technically sophisticated was the work of Margaret de Patta (1903–64). Influenced by Bauhaus principles (she had studied with Moholy-Nagy), her jewelry of the 1940s and 1950s consists

157

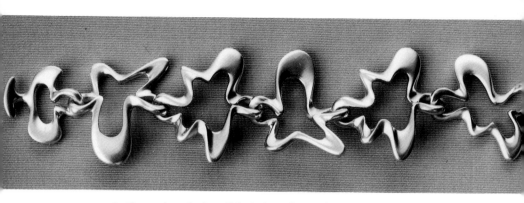

158 Abstract bracelet in polished silver, designed in 1947 by the sculptor Henning Koppel for Georg Jensen.

of stark geometric arrangements of metal and semi-precious stones. She developed new ways of setting stones so they appeared to float unsupported, and new cuts which gave unusual effects.

158   A distinctive sculptural style of jewelry emerged in Denmark after the war, led chiefly by the sculptor Henning Koppel (1918–1981). By the 1950s the other notable designers were Sigurd Perrson (b. 1914), Jørgen Ditzel (1921–61) and Nanna Ditzel (b. 1923), Bent Gabrielsen Pedersen (b. 1928) and the Swede Torun Bülow-Hübe (b. 1927). They created strong, softly rounded abstract shapes, usually cast in silver and sometimes decorated with a solid block of enamel colour or with semi-precious stones such as amethyst and rock crystal. Most of them worked at some point for Georg Jensen, the firm which came to represent for many the simplicity of Scandinavian design. The most effective styles were highly influential and remained in production for many years. The movement away from elaborate decoration to subtly constructed, minimal forms spread through Europe and America, and prepared the ground for the experimental jewelry of the 1960s and 1970s.

CHAPTER NINE

Since 1960

Jewelry has undergone a dramatic change since 1960. Whilst the major international houses have continued to work in precious materials following styles evolved from those of preceding decades, innovation has come in the main from individual artist-craftsmen trained at art schools. Often approaching their work more as a means of self-expression than as a commercial venture, they have challenged the notion of what jewelry is, through the use of new materials or through radically different forms. A multiplicity of new ideas have developed in parallel over a short period of time – some revolutionary in almost every respect, others in new styles but more clearly evolved from established traditions. Much of this work is still too recent for a definitive view to be possible on which new directions will have the most lasting importance, and what follows is of necessity a personal selection.

The new generation emerging in the 1960s and 1970s questioned the nature of jewelry and its role in society, and as in other art forms, accepted conventions were pushed aside. Many of the most talented graduates rejected what they considered to be status-laden jewelry bound by sexual stereotypes or contaminated by exploitation, in favour of the equality conveyed by materials of almost no intrinsic worth. The boundaries where jewelry approaches sculpture, clothing or even performance art were explored, and it became a medium for artistic experiment rather than simple adornment. Encouraged by increasing levels of affluence amongst ever more adventurous customers, a great deal of controversial work was made. In Germany this was fostered by the opening of the Schmuckmuseum (Jewelry Museum) in Pforzheim in 1961, while in London in the same year Goldsmiths Hall organized the first serious exhibition to include the new jewelry, showing over one thousand objects from twenty-eight countries. Commercial galleries contributed to the international exchange of ideas, notably the Electrum Gallery in London and Galerie Ra in Amsterdam, founded in 1971 and 1976 respectively.

Emmy van Leersum (1930–1984) and her husband Gijs Bakker (b. 1942) were amongst the most inventive jewellers of the late 1960s and early 1970s, dominating the scene in Holland and strongly influencing developments in the rest of Europe and America. They approached jewelry as 'sculpture to wear', the title of their 1966–67 joint exhibition in Amsterdam and London, and made simple, abstract neckpieces and bracelets which were intended to work with the wearer's body and clothing rather than impose any additional constraints. Both were committed to the idea that jewelry should promote equality, and therefore worked in non-precious materials such as aluminium and plastics. Their ideas became so entrenched amongst radical Dutch jewellers that the adoption of coloured golds by Robert Smit (b. 1941) in the mid-1980s was seen by his peers as shocking. Although Bakker now works mainly as an industrial designer, he continues to make jewelry, and is best known for his large neckpieces of laminated clear plastic with flat decoration set between the layers: a photographic image, pressed flower petals or sheets of gold leaf. He has recently begun to incorporate

159

159 Neckpiece by Gijs Bakker, consisting of a spiral of plastic set with petals plucked from a dahlia, 1986.

160 One from a series of brooches made by Otto Künzli in 1983 from hardfoam covered in different patterns of wallpaper.

diamonds in these compositions, on the grounds that society is now more equal than when he rejected precious materials in the 1960s.

Radical jewellers have continued to provoke debate, and Otto Künzli (b. Switzerland 1948) is one of the most thoughtful, controversial and technically skilled. In the early 1980s his large brooches of polystyrene 160 blocks covered in wallpaper raised the issue of how far jewelry can depart from expected forms and functions and still be defined as jewelry. He too dislikes the display of wealth: in his bangle entitled 'gold makes you blind', a ball of real gold is completely hidden, embedded within a band of black rubber. Social or political comment is more overt in the work of the Swiss jeweller Bernhard Schobinger (b. 1946), whose statements include a necklace made in 1990 of necks from broken bottles threaded on a cord. Examining the relationship between jewelry and the body, Schobinger's compatriot Pierre Degen (b. 1947) creates airy structures from ladders and poles of wood, which many feel should be seen rather as sculptures or performance pieces.

A wide range of new materials have been introduced to the jeweller's repertoire. The creative use of plastic, exploring its properties for their own sake rather than in imitation of other more valuable materials, was advanced in the 1960s by Van Leersum and Bakker. From the beginning of the 1970s Claus Bury (b. Germany 1946), Fritz Maierhofer (b. Austria 1941), Gerd Rothman (b. Germany 1941) and David Watkins (b. Britain 1940) were juxtaposing acrylic with finely worked precious metals, while in Australia Helge Larsen (b. 1929) and Darani Lewers (b. 1936) were using corrugated perspex to cover photographic images in silver pendants. Paper, one of the most ephemeral of materials, was used in the mid-1960s in Britain by Wendy Ramshaw (b. 1939) and David Watkins for a range of colourful jewelry called 'Something Special' which was sold flat and assembled by the purchaser. More recently Nel Linssen (b. The Netherlands 1935) has made substantial necklaces and bracelets from pleated paper. As papier-mâché, it has been used to make large sculptural pieces, from the vibrantly coloured 'paintings to wear' of the American Marjorie Schick (b. 1941) to the work of the Swiss-born but French-based Gilles Jonemann (b. 1944) with its soft matt tones.

In the late 1970s and early 1980s many jewellers looked towards textile fibres and fabrics as non-precious materials which could create softer forms than metal or plastic. Caroline Broadhead (b. 1950) made soft, chunky necklaces of twisted and bound cotton before moving on to long tufts of nylon filament fixed into a solid, plain neck piece or bracelet frame. In 1981 she began to weave coloured nylon line into flexible tubes which could be worn as a bulky necklace or extended upwards to form a long cowl hood. Other British jewellers exploring the area where jewelry overlaps with clothing included Susanna Heron (b. 1949) and Julia Manheim (b. 1949). These three jewellers classified their work as 'wearables', and have moved increasingly towards garments, hats and sculpture. In the early 1980s, the Dutch jeweller Lam de Wolf (b. 1949) experimented with multi-strand necklaces of shredded, wound or knotted fabric which were worn over the shoulder cascading down the back, and could also serve as wall-hangings.

161 Bracelet of pleated paper with a changeable form, by Nel Linssen, *c.* 1987.

The use of discarded things is a natural extension of the search for alternative materials, and as a form of recycling reflects current ecological concerns. Two jewellers who used 'found' objects deliberately from the mid-1960s were the Americans Fred Woell (b. 1934) and Robert Ebendorf (b. 1938), who made collage-like or 'assemblage' pieces. The theme has been widely explored, with recent variations by the American ROY (b. 1962) whose work incorporates panels cut from traffic signs, 163 and the Australian Susan Cohn (b. 1952) who makes brooches and hair-beads out of crushed pieces of metal ranging from aluminium mesh to fabricated gem-set jewelry, compressed into a rigid form. Recycling with a subtlety that disguises rather than emphasizes the origin of the materials underlies the work of two British jewellers. From the 1970s Malcolm Appleby (b. 1946) has recycled old gun barrels and cart wheels to make rings which he lines, edges and inlays with gold. Peter Chang (b. 1944) uses acrylic signboard off-cuts, shaped and set in colourful lacquer, to create psychedelic brooches and bracelets.

Reclaimed from nature rather than recycled, pebbles and seashells remain amongst the most satisfying of alternative materials used in jewelry. The French sculptor Jean Arp (1888–1966) recognized this with a brooch he designed around 1960 which was a pebble set in an abstract silver shape. In the mid-1960s Helga Zahn (1936–85), who was born in Germany but worked in England, framed smooth black Cornish pebbles with simple silver surrounds. A much rougher effect was achieved by the Munich-based South African Daniel Kruger (b. 1951) whose innovative work includes pendants of irregular, rough stones partially wrapped in gold foil. He has also used feathers, while Simon Costin (b. 1962) in Britain preserves the subtle markings of fish and reptiles by taxidermy, or incorporates the fragile beauty of small animal skulls.

The use of the human body has been explored too, with Gerd Rothmann's 'bodyprints'. Examples from the 1980s include an earring cast from the lower half of an ear which slots perfectly over a real ear, and a signet ring decorated with a real thumbprint. Heated debate was provoked by Gijs Bakker's invisible jewelry, such as his 1973 'bracelet' which was in fact the imprint left on the skin by a gold wire worn tightly on the arm. Body-piercing in its various forms, long established in some parts of the world, also influenced jewellers' work.

New ways have been developed to create intense colour. The thin film of oxide which covers titanium, tantalum and niobium can be transformed into a spectacular range of iridescent refracted colours when the metal is anodized. The effect has been exploited since the 1970s, notably by Edward de Large (b. 1945) who made brooches with futuristic and illusionist perspectives, and Alan Craxford (b. 1946) who further decorated pieces with engraving. Also in Britain, Jane Adam (b. 1959) reintroduced aluminium to jewelry in anodized and painted form, while Geoff Roberts (b. 1953) creates large and humorous pieces out of brightly coloured metal foil. Moving away from metals, the sculptor Andrew Logan (b. 1945) has developed a distinctive technique of setting fragments of coloured mirror glass into resin. Also working on a large scale, Annie Sherburne (b. 1957) makes exuberant jewelry from painted wood set with coloured glass stones.

162 Brooch by Peter Chang,
1992. Diverse plastic elements
are fixed to an inner wooden
core, the spaces between are
filled with lacquer, and then
the piece is polished to achieve
a seamless finish.

163 'American Dream' bracelet,
by ROY, 1993, in which a traffic
'STOP' sign is recycled, set in silver
with diamonds and a ruby.

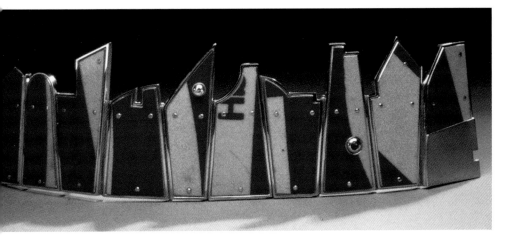

Although the work of the most controversial jewellers remained too academic and remote for widespread popular appeal, innovation has sometimes been promoted by the world of *haute couture*. Amongst British fashion designers, Rifat Ozbek has used Peter Chang's work; Zandra Rhodes, Andrew Logan's; and Antony Price that of the Irish sculptor and jeweller Slim Barrett (b. 1960). In America, Donna Karan selected pieces in matt and patinated brass by jeweller and gallery owner Robert Lee Morris (b. 1947). Chanel's reputation for high quality costume jewelry has been maintained under the direction of Karl Lagerfeld, while surrealism reminiscent of Schiaparelli has characterized the work of collector and designer Billy Boy. Since 1987 Christian Lacroix has encouraged extravagant costume jewelry, notably the Lacroix Cross.

Many artist-jewellers working since 1960 have preferred to express their ideas in traditional materials, developing different approaches and techniques for precious metals, often with less emphasis on faceted gemstones. There have also been influences from painting and sculpture, and Modernist ideas developed from the Bauhaus have continued to provide inspiration.

Established painters and sculptors have made a significant contribution in the years since the war. Salvador Dalí (1904–89) had designed flamboyant Surrealist jewelry in the late 1940s and 1950s, most famously the 'Eye of Time' watch brooch (1949). Georges Braque (1882–1963) collaborated with Heger de Löwenfeld to create a collection of brooches in the early 1960s. These translated themes from his paintings, notably a bird in flight, into textured gold, pavé-set diamonds and blocks of lapis lazuli or red jasper. Pablo Picasso (1881–1973), Jean Cocteau (1891–1963) and Max Ernst (1891–1976) made models which were then cast in gold as medallions and brooches. In Britain the painter Alan Davie (b. 1920) began making jewelry in the mid-1950s, influenced by Pre-Columbian ornament and primitive forms. Several contemporary artists, including Kenneth Armitage (b. 1916), Elisabeth Frink (1930–93), Terry Frost (b. 1915) and William Scott (1913–89), contributed pieces to the 1961 exhibition at Goldsmiths Hall in London.

The influence of Abstract Expressionist painters such as Jackson Pollock was felt in jewelry design in the early 1960s. Two London 164 jewellers, John Donald (b. 1928) and Andrew Grima (b. 1921), designed some of the most dramatic pieces in this new asymmetrical style. Their abstract forms with irregular, splintered profiles were often inspired by nature, and at times appeared to have been formed by an untamed natural process rather than by design. The textured gold surfaces were in some cases made by taking impressions from real leaves and bark, and

164 Rough-textured gold and asymmetrical splintered forms became fashionable during the early 1960s. Andrew Grima was at the forefront of this new style: he designed this brooch, of yellow gold and diamonds, in 1963.

the stones chosen included large and unusual mineral samples such as agate geodes and jagged quartz crystals, as well as opals, tourmalines and scatterings of diamonds.

Amongst those who continued to work with precious metals, great attention was devoted to discovering new surface textures and patinas. In Germany Elisabeth Treskow (b. 1898) had after extensive experimentation rediscovered the Etruscan technique of granulation around 1930 (preceded independently by the Munich goldsmith Johann Wilm), and used it on abstract pieces in the 1950s and 1960s. Reinhold Reiling (1922–83) was influential in the development of a new style of German jewelry in the 1960s, using matt and textured gold in softened geometric and abstract forms. In Britain Breon O'Casey (b. 1928) had begun to

169

166

165 Detail of a necklace by
Gerda Flöckinger, made in
two parts in 1975 and 1986.
The rich surface texture
(seen approximately actual
size) combines oxidized
silver, gold, opals,
diamonds and pearls; the
clasp is of polished quartz.

166 Brooch of gold set with
a ruby and a diamond, by
Reinhold Reiling, 1967.

produce work inspired by ancient and ethnic jewelry in 1960, using unpolished precious metals which have a hand-beaten irregularity, some-times complemented by semi–precious stones left with a frosted finish. In America Earl Pardon (1926–91) also explored surface texture, and established his position of influence as a craftsman and teacher.

In Britain Gerda Flöckinger (b. 1927 in Austria) began to develop a distinctive encrusted finish in the second half of the 1960s, covering the surface with apparently molten spirals, spheres, bubbles and holes. Much of her early work is in silver, set asymmetrically with turquoises and cabochon stones. The pieces have gradually become more delicate and opulent, combining swirling gold with white or oxidized silver, set with opals, pearls and scatterings of tiny diamonds. In 1962 she established the first British course in experimental jewelry, at Hornsey School of Art

165

167 Neckpiece by Kazuhiro Itoh, 1992, made of cypress wood shavings held together with knotted lengths of steel wire.

in London. Jacqueline Mina (b. 1942) has concentrated on contrasts of texture and colour in gold and platinum, using techniques such as *samorodok* (where the surface of the gold is gently roughened by being melted), and later the Japanese colouring technique of *mokume gane* or 'wood grain metal' (where layers of coloured golds are repeatedly rolled and cut to create an abstract marbled effect). Recent work includes the inlaying of platinum mesh into gold to create the effect of brocade.

Most of the major Italian jewellers have continued working with gold, regardless of the debates elsewhere in Europe, and in Padua particularly a relaxed and elegant abstract style has developed in lustrous matt gold, almost always without gemstones. During the professorship of Mario Pinton (b. 1919) at the Istituto Statale d'Arte and Istituto d'Arte 'Pietro 169
Selvatico' the city became the leading centre for artistic jewelry in Italy.
He was followed by Giampaolo Babetto (b. 1947), whose pieces are based 169
on three-dimensional geometric forms, occasionally incorporating niello or a coloured acrylic resin. Francesco Pavan (b. 1937) has used similar shapes, but has introduced more surface complexity.

In Japan after the Second World War a small number of young goldsmiths emerged, who were influenced by trends in Europe but were at the same time imbued with distinctly national cultural themes and minimalism. Foremost amongst them is Yasuki Hiramatsu (b. 1926), who 169
through his works and his teaching at Tokyo University has promoted Japanese jewelry at home and abroad. Gold and silver foil is given depth by being layered or crumpled, and ribbons of thicker metal are massed together in necklaces and bracelets, with surface texture again a major element of the design. Kazuhiro Itoh (b. 1948) made angular rings in gold set with marble slabs in the 1970s, but by the late 1980s had moved away from conventional materials to bamboo twigs arranged in clear plastic pockets. More recently he has devised collars of curved wood-shavings, 167
fastened together with steel wire.

Wire, made from precious or base metals, has been used in a variety of new ways, to create both the structure of a piece and the decoration on its surface. In some cases the result is a flexible, open tracery of loops, while in others the wires are closely packed in a rigid formation. Textile techniques such as knitting, weaving and crochet have been adapted by jewellers working in precious metals. In America Arline Fisch (b. 1931) 170
made loosely hand-knitted bracelets in the 1970s, while weaving in 170
fine-gauge wire was pioneered by Mary Lee Hu (b. 1943): using a single colour, she achieves varied textures through the pattern of the weave. In Britain crocheted wire is used by Susan Cross (b. 1964), while 170
Catherine Martin has adapted the traditional Japanese braiding technique 170

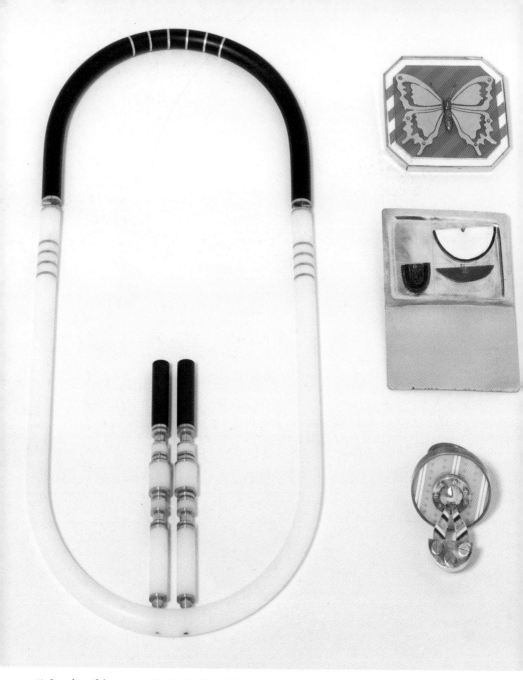

168 Jewelry of the 1970s: (clockwise from left) neckpiece by David Watkins, of acrylic and gold, 1975; brooch by Gerd Rothmann, of steel and acrylic, 1970; brooch by Anton Cepka, of silver and enamel, c. 1972; ring by Fritz Maierhofer, of silver and acrylic, 1973.

169 New ideas in traditional materials: (top) gold neckpiece by Mario Pinton, 1961; (above left) fish brooch of gold with granulation, set with a sapphire, a pearl and diamonds, by Elisabeth Treskow, 1953; (above right) 'Athene Noctua' brooch by Kevin Coates, of gold, platinum, titanium and oxidized silver, 1983; (below left) brooch by Yasuki Hiramatsu, of crumpled gold, 1990; (centre) 'The Virgin and the Unicorn' brooch by William Harper, of gold, silver, enamel, pearls, tourmalines and an amethyst crystal, 1988; (below right) gold ring by Giampaolo Babetto, 1980.

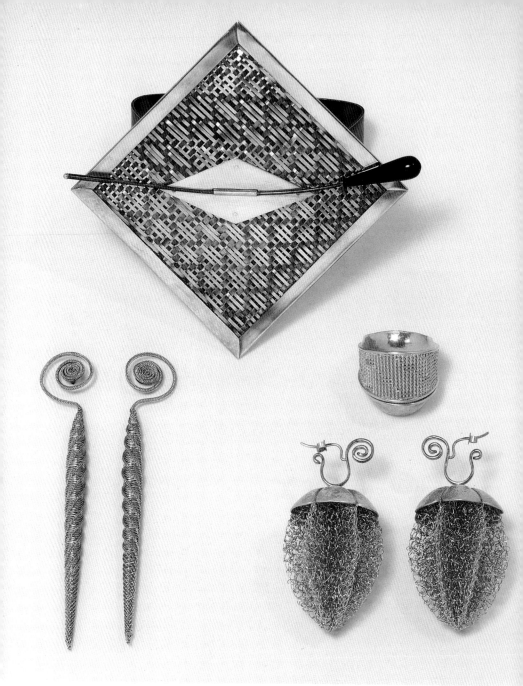

170 Textile techniques explored in metal wire: (top) bracelet by Arline Fisch, with a woven panel of coloured golds that can be detached and worn as a brooch, 1987; (below left) earrings by Catherine Martin, of platinum, braided according to classical Japanese techniques, 1991; (right, centre) ring by Mary Lee Hu, with a panel of woven gold, *c.* 1990; (right, below) earrings by Susan Cross, of crocheted platinum and gold wire, 1988.

of *kumihimo*. Esther Ward (b. 1964) works mainly in stainless steel wire, from which she devises a series of identical linear forms, jointed to fall in different shapes as the piece is worn. The Australian Carlier Makigawa (b. 1952) uses wire to create hollow three-dimensional structures made from gracefully curving lines.

Enamel remains an important decorative technique, with Jane Short (b. 1954) in Britain producing detailed and subtly coloured *basse-taille* pieces. The American craftsman William Harper (b. 1944) uses vivid *cloisonné* enamel with rough-textured gold, mineral crystals and baroque pearls to create fantastical compositions which usually have a symbolic meaning behind their abstract form. Very different enamel effects distinguish the work of his compatriot Jamie Bennett (b. 1948), who developed a granular opaque enamel encrusted in different colours over the entire surface of his jewels.

The ideas of the Modernists, dating back to the Bauhaus and beyond, have continued to inspire jewellers in recent decades. In Britain, Wendy Ramshaw gained the Council of Industrial Design Award in 1972, and has continued to create Modernist, and recently Postmodernist, classics in a wide range of materials and to the highest technical standards. She invented ring sets, sometimes with more than ten rings to be worn together, boldly combining colours and shapes (which often extend beyond the line of the finger), and inviting the wearer to create endless variations. Sold with display stands, the sets function both as jewelry and as small sculpture. In recent years she has used themes drawn from the many paintings of women by Picasso, in a series called 'Picasso's Ladies'.

Hermann Jünger (b. 1928), formerly professor of jewelry at the Akademie der Bildenden Künste in Munich, has produced abstract compositions in precious metals since the mid-1960s. His pieces are usually first worked out in watercolour and line drawings, and reflect the Bauhaus ideal of keeping design to its essentials. He too has promoted the idea of jewelry which invites the wearer's participation and which is designed to be displayed when not being worn. By the end of the 1970s he was making necklaces whose component parts – geometric beads of different shapes in a variety of metals and coloured hardstones – may be assembled on a simple gold wire according to the wearer's wishes. He presents these pieces in display boxes with a separate compartment for each element.

Abstract sculptural forms characterize the work of Onno Boekhoudt (b. 1944) in The Netherlands, much of which is inspired indirectly by nature: a brooch of 1980 made of silver repeatedly sawed into strips and

169

171

172

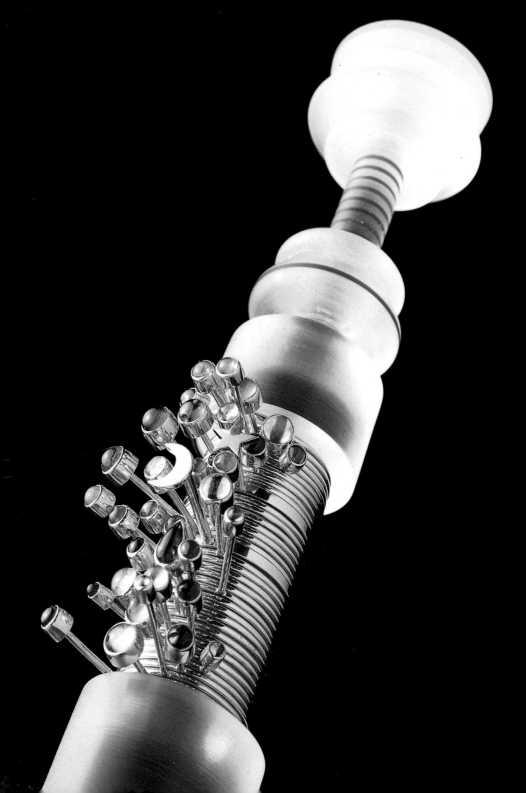

172 Boxed necklace set by Hermann Jünger, 1990. The geometric forms, made of
silver, silver-gilt, lapis lazuli, chalcedony, haematite and granite, are designed to be
threaded onto the gold wire according to the wishes of the wearer. When not
being worn, the elements in their box can be enjoyed as sculpture.

171 *opposite* Ring set of forty rings by Wendy Ramshaw, 1988, inspired by
Picasso's painting *The Dream*. The rings are made of gold set with garnet, sapphire,
moonstone, tourmaline, labradorite and amethyst. They are displayed on a
characteristic stand of turned perspex. In this case the set is not all intended for
the same finger, but is to be divided between several fingers.

soldered back together has a texture that is curiously geological, and he has also experimented with sections of tree trunks as enlarged models for rings. In Britain, the jewelry of Elisabeth Holder (b. 1950 in Germany) exhibits a similar simplicity of form and thoughtfulness of approach, although it is more geometric; while Cynthia Cousens (b. 1956) has developed a restrained and sculptural style enhanced with subtle surface treatments.

Technology has been a recurring influence in design during recent decades. The work of David Watkins, of the Royal College of Art, London, is typified by extreme simplicity and precise forms which often draw on technological imagery. Most characteristic are his neckpieces, consisting of coloured acrylic rods inlaid with bands of metal and with precise hinges and joints, or alternatively multiple circles of fine steel wire with decorative geometric attachments all coated in vividly coloured neoprene.

Friedrich Becker (b. 1922) in Germany worked as an engine fitter and studied aeronautics before turning to jewelry. Undecorated surfaces in turned steel or white gold are characteristic of his work, and he is particularly noted for rings and bracelets which include moving parts – 'kinetic jewelry'. The ability of his forms to glide on their axes with unexpected rapidity relies on the technical excellence of the joints and micro-ball-bearings concealed within the piece.

Technology has influenced many other jewellers, including Claus Bury, Gerd Rothmann and Fritz Maierhofer, who incorporated abstract forms inspired by engineering components into their work. The Slovak Anton Cepka (b. 1936) exploited the imagery of radar and radio installations, moving from flat coloured elements riveted onto panels of untreated silver to lattice outlines which show the objects' underlying structures. Frank Bauer (b. 1942 in Germany but active in Australia) has worked with three-dimensional metal frameworks, producing angular geometric constructions with a mathematical precision and purity of form. The potential of computer-aided design has been explored in recent years, notably by David Watkins and by the American jeweller Stanley Lechtzin (b. 1936), whose interest in technology includes earlier experiments with electroforming – the electrical depositing of metal on a non-metallic surface.

A few jewellers have adopted the idea of unit construction, creating pieces from a number of smaller, identical linked elements. In Britain in the 1960s Patricia Meyerowitz was using machine off-cuts and industrial waste in this way. The Norwegian Tone Vigeland (b. 1938) uses metal links to create a supple chain mail, to which in her earlier work she

173 Time-lapse photograph of a kinetic ring by Friedrich Becker, made in 1982 from geometric sections of steel, showing the motion produced by the pivoting sections of the bezel.

attached a feather-like covering made of beaten steel drops and long gold beads. Her later work is starker, with the units made of flat geometric shapes, usually in sombre patinated metal.

Although modern jewelry has tended to take abstract forms, important naturalistic pieces continue to be made. Since the later 1960s Charlotte de Syllas (b. 1946) has carved intricate shapes based on natural forms in subtly coloured hardstones and coral. Again in Britain, symbolism and hidden meanings have inspired Kevin Coates (b. 1950) to create jewelry which is often figurative – drawing on ideas from mythology, literature, music, mathematics and the subconscious – and which also combines an impressive variety of materials and techniques.

169

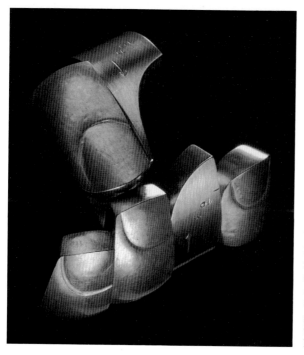

174 'Metamorphosis' bracelet
by Bruno Martinazzi, 1992. The
hand and the measuring device
represent aspects of the physical
and the conceptual. Two different
colours and strengths of gold are
used: the fingers are of soft, yellow
gold with a beaten finish, while
the measure is of a polished,
harder and paler gold.

174   Bruno Martinazzi (b. 1923) of Turin has produced finely modelled jewelry which, like his large sculptures, is based on parts of the human body and illustrates the different senses. His approach is strongly influenced by philosophical ideas: finger and hand pieces explore notions of creativity and friendship, while measuring devices – carefully arranged lines and numbers – represent ways in which man has tried to understand the universe around him.

Since the 1960s, jewelry has generated debate about what materials it should be made from, how its boundaries should be defined, and whether it is art. Prejudices over materials and techniques have been largely overcome. The boundaries between jewelry, sculpture, performance art and fashion have been stretched and will continue to be redefined by artists not wishing to be constrained by convention. What remains true now, as throughout the ages, is that jewelry at its finest has the power to fascinate and inspire – which is the prime characteristic of art at its best in any of its many manifestations.

Bibliography

General

Addison, K. J. and S., *Pearls. Ornament and Obsession*, 1992

Antwerp: Koningin Fabiolalazaal, *The Jewel – Sign and Symbol*, exh., 1995

Balfour, I., *Famous Diamonds*, 1987

Baltimore, Md: Walters Art Gallery, *Jewelry. Ancient to Modern*, 1979

Becker, V., *Fabulous Fakes*, 1988

Black, A. J., *A History of Jewels*, 1981

Boardman, J., and D. Scarisbrick, *The Ralph Harari Collection of Finger Rings*, 1977

Bury, S., *Jewellery Gallery Summary Catalogue* [Victoria & Albert Museum, London], 1982

— *An Introduction to Rings*, 1984

Chadour, A. B., *Rings. The Alice and Louis Koch Collection. Forty Centuries seen by Four Generations*, 1994

— and R. Joppien, *Schmuck I & II* [Kunstgewerbemuseum, Cologne], 1985

Dalgleish, G., and R. Marshall, *The Art of Jewellery in Scotland*, exh., Scottish National Portrait Gallery, Edinburgh, 1991

Dalton, O. M., *Catalogue of the Finger Rings, Early Christian, Byzantine, Teutonic, Medieval and Later. Franks Bequest* [British Museum, London], 1912

D'Orey, L., *Five Centuries of Jewellery. National Museum of Ancient Art, Lisbon*, 1995

Dubin, L. S., *History of Beads*, 1987

Egger, G., *Bürgerlicher Schmuck*, 1984

Evans, J., *English Jewellery from the Fifth Century AD to 1800*, 1921

— *A History of Jewellery, 1100–1870*, 1970

Fales Gandy, M., *Jewelry in America*, 1995

Fraquet, H., *Amber*, 1987

Gregoretti, G., *Jewellery through the Ages*, 1970

Henig, M., D. Scarisbrick and M. Whiting, *Classical Gems: Ancient and Modern Intaglios and Cameos in the Fitzwilliam Museum* [Cambridge], 1994

Hinks, P., *Jewellery*, 1969

Hughes, G., *The Art of Jewelry*, 1972

Jonas, S., and M. Nissenson, *Cuff Links*, 1991

Lanllier, J., and M.-A. Pini, *Cinq Siècles de Joaillerie en Occident*, 1971

Lewis, M. D. S., *Antique Paste Jewellery*, 1970

London: Museum of London, *Treasures and Trinkets. Jewellery in London from Pre-Roman Times to the 1930s*, exh., 1991

London: Natural History Museum, *Gemstones*, 1987

Mascetti, D., and A. Triossi, *Earrings from Antiquity to the Present*, 1990

Medvedeva, G., et al., *Russian Jewellery 16th–20th Centuries. From the Collection of the Historical Museum, Moscow*, 1987

Morel, B., *The French Crown Jewels*, 1988

Muller, H., *Jet*, 1987

Munn, G. C., *The Triumph of Love. Jewelry 1530–1930*, 1993

New York: Metropolitan Museum of Art, *Metropolitan Jewelry*, 1991

Newman, H., *An Illustrated Dictionary of Jewelry*, 1981

Ogden, J., et al., *Jewellery. Makers, Motifs, History, Techniques*, 1989

Oman, C. C., *Catalogue of Rings* [Victoria & Albert Museum, London], 1930

— *British Rings 800–1914*, 1974

Oved, S., *The Book of Necklaces*, 1953

Proddow, P., and D. Healy, *American Jewelry. Glamour and Tradition*, 1987

Scarisbrick, D., *Ancestral Jewels*, 1989

— *Rings. Symbols of Wealth, Power and Affection*, 1993

— *Jewellery in Britain 1066–1837*, 1994

Schiffer, N., *Costume Jewelry – the Fun of Collecting*, 1988

— *The Power of Jewelry*, 1988

Society of Jewellery Historians, London, *Jewellery Studies*

Tait, H., ed., *Jewellery through 7000 years* [British Museum, London], 1976

—, T. Wilson, J. Rudoe and C. Gere, *The Art of the Jeweller. A Catalogue of the Hull Grundy Gift to the British Museum* [London], 1984

Taylor, G., and D. Scarisbrick, *Finger Rings from Ancient Egypt to the Present Day*, exh., Ashmolean Museum, Oxford, 1978

Thage, J., *Danish Jewelry*, 1990

Tillander, H., *Diamond Cuts in Historic Jewellery 1381–1910*, 1995

Twining, E. F., *A History of the Crown Jewels of Europe*, 1960

Untracht, O., *Jewelry Concepts and Technology*, 1982

Vasconcelos e Sousa, D. G. de, *Reais Joias no Norte de Portugal*, exh., Palacio da Bolsa, Porto, 1995

Ward, A., J. Cherry, C. Gere and B. Cartlidge, *The Ring from Antiquity to the Twentieth Century*, 1981

Zucker, B., *Gems and Jewels*, 1984

1 The Ancient World

Aldred, C., *Jewels of the Pharaohs*, 1971

Andrews, C., *Ancient Egyptian Jewellery*, 1990

Bland, R., and C. Johns, *The Hoxne Treasure*, 1993

Boardman, J., *Greek Gems and Finger Rings*, 1970

Higgins, R. A., *Greek and Roman Jewellery*, 1961/1980

— *The Aegina Treasure. An Archaeological Mystery*, 1979

Marshall, F. H., *Catalogue of the Finger Rings, Greek, Etruscan and Roman, in the Departments of Antiquities, British Museum* [London], 1907

— *Catalogue of the Greek, Etruscan and Roman Jewellery in the British Museum* [London], 1911

New York: Metropolitan Museum of Art, *Treasures of Early Irish Art*, exh., 1977

Ogden, J., *Jewellery of the Ancient World*, 1982

— *Ancient Jewellery*, 1992

Pforzheim: Schmuckmuseum, *Gold aus Griechenland*, exh., 1992

Richter, G. M., *The Engraved Gems of the Greeks, Etruscans and Romans*, 1968–71

Wilkinson, A., *Ancient Egyptian Jewellery*, 1971

Williams, D., and J. Ogden, *Greek Gold*, exh., 1994

2 Byzantium and Early Europe

Bank, A., *Byzantine Art in the Collections of Soviet Museums*, 1977

Brussels: Musées Royaux d'Art et d'Histoire, *Splendeur de Byzance*, exh., 1982

Buckton, D., ed., *Byzantium. Treasures of Byzantine Art and Culture*, exh., British Museum, London, 1994

Dodwell, C., *Anglo-Saxon Art. A New Perspective*, 1982

Evans, A. C., *Sutton Hoo Ship Burial*, 1986

217

Jessup, R., *Anglo-Saxon Jewellery*, 1974
Loverance, R., *Byzantium*, 1994
Megaw, R. and V., *Celtic Art. From its Beginnings to the Book of Kells*, 1990
Ross, M., *Catalogue of the Byzantine and Early Medieval Antiquities in the Dumbarton Oaks Collection* [Washington, D. C.], *Vol. II: Jewelry, Enamels and the Art of the Migration Period*, 1965
Ryan, M., *Metal Craftsmanship in Early Ireland*, 1993
Stead, I. M., *Celtic Art*, 1985
Webster, L., and J. Backhouse, eds, *The Making of England, Anglo-Saxon Art and Culture AD 600–900*, exh., British Museum, London, 1991
Weitzmann, K., ed., *The Age of Spirituality. Late Antique and Early Christian Art, Third to Seventh Century*, exh., Metropolitan Museum, New York, 1979
Wessel, K., *Byzantine Enamels*, 1969
Wilson, D., *The Anglo-Saxons*, 1981
Youngs, S., ed., *The Work of Angels. Masterpieces of Celtic Metalwork, 6th–9th Centuries AD*, exh., 1989

3 The Middle Ages

Alexander, J., and P. Binski, eds, *The Age of Chivalry. Art in Plantagenet England 1200–1400*, exh., Royal Academy, London, 1987
Campbell, M., *An Introduction to Medieval Enamels*, 1983
— 'Gold, Silver and Precious Stones' in *English Medieval Industries*, ed. J. Blair and N. Ramsay, 1991
Cherry, J., *Medieval Craftsmen: Goldsmiths*, 1992
Evans, J., *Magical Jewels of the Middle Ages and the Renaissance*, 1922
Fingerlin, I., *Gürtel des hohen und späten Mittelalters*, 1971
Gauthier, M.-M., *Émaux du Moyen Age occidental*, 1972
Lightbown, R., *Medieval European Jewellery*, 1992
London: Hayward Gallery, *English Romanesque Art 1066–1200*, exh., 1984
London: Museum of London, *Dress Accessories. Medieval Finds from Excavations in London*, 1991
Steingräber, E., *Alter Schmuck*, 1956
Taburet-Delahaye, E., *L'Orfèvrerie gothique au Musée de Cluny. XIIIe–début XVe siècle*, 1989

4 The Renaissance

Cellini, B., *Autobiography*, ed. and abr. C. Hope and A. Nova, 1983
Evans, J.: see section 3
Hackenbroch, Y., *Renaissance Jewellery*, 1979
—*Enseignes. Renaissance Hat Jewels*, 1996
Hearn, K., ed., *Dynasties. Painting in Tudor and Jacobean England 1530–1630*, exh., Tate Gallery, London, 1995
Lesley, P., *Renaissance Jewels and Jeweled Objects from the Melvin Gutman Collection*, 1968
London: Victoria & Albert Museum/ Debrett, *Princely Magnificence. Court Jewels of the Renaissance, 1500–1630*, exh., 1980
Muller, P., *Jewels in Spain 1500–1800*, 1972
Scarisbrick, D., *Tudor and Jacobean Jewellery*, 1995
Somers Cocks, A., *An Introduction to Courtly Jewellery*, 1980
— and C. Truman, *The Thyssen-Bornemisza Collection. Renaissance Jewels, Gold Boxes and Objets de Vertu*, 1995
Tait, H., *Catalogue of the Waddesdon Bequest in the British Museum* [London], *Vol. I, The Jewels*, 1986

5 Baroque to Revolution

Antwerp: Diamond Museum, *A Sparkling Age. 17th Century Diamond Jewellery*, exh., 1993
Bury, S., *An Introduction to Sentimental Jewellery*, 1985
—*Jewellery 1789–1910 – The International Era*, 1991
Chanlot, A., *Les Ouvrages en cheveux, leurs secrets*, 1986
Clifford, A., *Cut-steel and Berlin Iron Jewellery*, 1971
Cummins, G., and N. Taunton, *Chatelaines. Utility to Glorious Extravagance*, 1994
Gorewa, O., I. Polynina, N. Rachmanov and A. Raimann, *Joyaux du Trésor de Russie*, 1991
Hughes, B. and T., *Georgian Shoe Buckles. Illustrated by the Lady Maufe Collection of Shoe Buckles at Kenwood* [London], 1972
Marquardt, B., *Schmuck. Klassizismus und Biedermeier 1780–1850. Deutschland, Österreich, Schweiz*, 1983
Mould, P., *The English Shoe Buckle*, n.d.
Muller, P.: see section 4

Northampton Museum, *Catalogue of Shoe and Other Buckles*, 1981
Scarisbrick, D., *Chaumet*, 1995

6 The Nineteenth Century

Baarsen, R., and G. Van Berge, *Jewellery 1820–1920*, [Rijksmuseum, Amsterdam], 1990
Becker, V., *Antique and 20th Century Jewellery*, 1980
Bennet, D., and D. Mascetti, *Understanding Jewellery*, 1989
Bury, S.: see section 5
Cavill, K., G. Cocks and J. Grace, *Australian Jewellers, Gold and Silversmiths – Makers and Marks*, 1992
Chanlot, A.: see section 5
Clifford, A.: see section 5
Cooper, D., and N. Battershill, *Victorian Sentimental Jewellery*, 1972
Cummins, G., and N. Taunton: see section 5
Ettinger, R., *Popular Jewelry 1840–1940*, 1990
Flower, M., *Victorian Jewellery*, 1951, rev. edn 1967
Gere, C., *Victorian Jewellery Design*, 1972
— *European and American Jewellery 1830–1914*, 1975
— and G. C. Munn, *Artists' Jewellery: From the Pre-Raphaelites to the Arts and Crafts Movement*, 1989
Hinks, P., *Nineteenth Century Jewellery*, 1975
—*Victorian Jewellery. A Complete Compendium of over Four Thousand Pieces of Jewellery*, 1991
Koch, M., et al., *The Belle Époque of French Jewellery 1850–1910*, 1991
Köchert, I. H., *Köchert Jewellery Designs 1810–1940*, 1990
Marquardt, B.: see section 5
Munn, G. C., *Castellani and Giuliano*, 1984
Néret, G., *Boucheron*, 1988
New York: Bard Graduate Centre, *Cast Iron from Central Europe 1800–1850*, exh., 1994
New York: Metropolitan Museum of Art, *The Age of Napoleon*, exh., 1989
O'Day, D., *Victorian Jewellery*, 1974
Rainwater, D. T., *American Jewelry Manufacturers*, 1988
Scarisbrick, D.: see section 5
Schofield, A., and K. Fahy, *Australian Jewellery – 19th and Early 20th Century*, 1991
Solodkoff, A., *Russian Gold and Silver*, 1981

Vever, H., *La Bijouterie française au XIXe siècle*, 1908
Zurich: Museum Bellerive, *De Fouquet 1860–1960 – Schmuck Künstler in Paris*, exh., 1984

7 The Belle Epoque

Bennet, D., and D. Mascetti: see section 6
Bainbridge, H. C., *Peter Carl Fabergé*, 1949
Barten, S., *René Lalique – Schmuck und Objets d'Art 1890–1910*, 1977
Becker, V., *Art Nouveau Jewellery*, 1985
— *The Jewellery of René Lalique*, exh., Goldsmiths' Hall, London, 1987
Bury, S., *Jewellery 1789–1910*: see section 5
Cumming, E., *Phoebe Anna Traquair 1852–1936*, exh., National Galleries of Scotland, Edinburgh, 1993
Ettinger, R.: see section 6
Gere, C., *European and American Jewellery*: see section 6
— and G. C. Munn: see section 6
Hapsburg, G. von, and M. Lopato, *Fabergé. Imperial Jeweller*, 1994
Hase, U. von, *Schmuck in Deutschland und Österreich 1895–1914*, 1977
Johnson, P., and P. Garner, eds, *Art Nouveau, The Anderson Collection* [Sainsbury Centre for Visual Arts, Norwich], n.d.
Karlin, E. Z., *Jewelry and Metalwork in the Arts and Crafts Tradition*, 1993
Koch, M., et al.: see section 6
Köchert, I. H.: see section 6
London: Victoria & Albert Museum, *Exhibition of Victorian and Edwardian Decorative Arts*, 1952
— *Liberty's 1875–1975*, exh., 1975
Martin, S., *Archibald Knox*, 1995
Mourey, G., A. Vallance et al., *Art Nouveau Jewellery and Fans*, 1973
Nadelhoffer, H., *Cartier*, 1984
Naylor, G., *The Arts and Crafts Movement*, 1971
Paris: Musée des Arts Décoratifs, *René Lalique. Bijoux, Verre*, exh., 1991
Scarisbrick, D.: see section 5
Schofield, A., and K. Fahy: see section 6
Snowman, A. K., *The Art of Carl Fabergé*, 1953
— ed., *The Master Jewelers*, 1990
Solodkoff, A.: see section 6
Tilbrook, A. J., and G. House, *The Designs of Archibald Knox for Liberty and Co.*, 1976
Vever, H.: see section 6

Zapata, J., *The Jewelry and Enamels of Louis Comfort Tiffany*, 1993
Zurich: Museum Bellerive: see section 6

8, 9 The 20th Century

General
Becker, V.: see section 6
Cartlidge, B., *Twentieth-Century Jewelry*, 1985
Cavill, K., G. Cocks and J. Grace: see section 6
Cera, D. F., ed., *Jewels of Fantasy. Costume Jewelry of the 20th Century*, 1992
Field, L., *The Jewels of Queen Elizabeth II. Her Personal Collection*, 1992
Hinks, P., *Twentieth Century British Jewellery 1900–1980*, 1983
Hughes, G., *Modern Jewelry, an International Survey 1890–1963*, 1963
Karlin, E. Z.: see section 6
Lenti, L., *Gioielli e gioiellieri di Valenza: Arte e storia orafa 1825–1975*, 1994
London: Worshipful Company of Goldsmiths, *International Exhibition of Modern Jewellery 1890–1961*, 1961
Mulvagh, J., *Costume Jewellery in Vogue*, 1988
Munich: Bayerisches Nationalmuseum, *Müncher Schmuck 1900–1940*, 1990
Néret, G.: see section 6
Proddow, P., D. Healy and Fasel, *Hollywood Jewels*, 1992
Pullée, C., *20th Century Jewelry*, 1990
Rainwater, D. T.: see section 6
Rühle-Diebener Publishers, *Schmuck von 1900 bis 1980 / Jewelry from 1900 to 1980*, 1982
Scarisbrick, D.: see section 6
Un Siglo de Joyería y Bisutería Española 1890–1990, exh., Institut Balear de Disseny, 1991
Snowman, A. K., ed., *The Master Jewelers*: see section 7
Vautrin, L., and P. Mauriès, *Line Vautrin. Sculptor, Jeweller, Magician*, 1992
Zurich: Museum Bellerive: see section 6

From Art Deco to the 1950s
Bennet, D., and D. Mascetti: see section 6
Ettinger, R.: see section 6
Gabardi, M., *Les Bijoux des années 50*, 1986
— *Art Deco Jewellery 1920–1949*, 1989
Hase-Schmund, U., C. Weber and I. Becker, *Theodor Fahmer – Jewellery between Avant-Garde and Tradition*, 1991

Menkes, S., *The Windsor Style*, 1987
Nadelhoffer, H.: see section 7
Raulet, S., *Art Deco Jewelry*, 1985
Rudolph, M., *Naum Slutzky. Meister am Bauhaus, Goldschmied und Designer*, 1990
Sotheby's, *The Jewels of the Duchess of Windsor*, sale cat., Geneva, April 1987
Weber, C., *Schmuck – der 20er und 30er Jahre in Deutschland*, 1990
Zurich: Museum Bellerive: see section 6

Since the 1960s
Anderson, P., *Contemporary Jewellery – The Australian Experience 1977–1987*, 1988
Crafts Council, London, *Crafts Magazine*
— *Shining Through*, exh., 1995
Dormer, P., and R. Turner, *The New Jewelry; Trends and Traditions*, 1985
Drutt English, H., and P. Dormer, *Jewelry of Our Time. Art, Ornament and Obsession*, 1995
Fitch, J., *The Art and Craft of Jewellery*, 1992
Ghent: Museum voor Sierkunst, *Japanese Contemporary Jewellery*, exh., 1995
Grant Lewin, S., *One of a Kind. American Art Jewelry Today*, 1994
Houston, J., *Caroline Broadhead. Jewellery in Studio*, 1990
Joppien, R., *Elisabeth Treskow*, exh., Museum für Angewandte Kunst, Cologne, 1990
London: Lesley Craze Gallery, *Today's Jewels. From Paper to Gold*, exh., 1993
London: Victoria & Albert Museum, *Wendy Ramshaw*, exh., 1982
— *Modern Artists' Jewels*, exh., 1984
— *Kevin Coates*, exh., 1985
— *Gerda Flöckinger*, exh., 1986
— *Fritz Maierhofer*, exh., 1988
Mainz: Landesmuseum, *Schmuckkunst der moderne Grossbritannien*, 1995
Manhart, T., *William Harper. Artist as Alchemist*, exh., Orlando Museum of Art, Fla., 1989
Meyerowitz, P., *Jewelry and Sculpture through Unit Construction*, 1967
Pforzheim: Schmuckmuseum, *Ornamenta 1*, exh., 1989
Scottish Arts Council, Edinburgh, *Jewellery in Europe*, exh., 1975
Turner, R., *Contemporary Jewelry, a Critical Assessment 1945–75*, 1976
Valcke, J., and P.-P. Dupont, *Contemporary Belgian Jewellery*, 1992
Watkins, D., *The Best in Contemporary Jewellery*, 1993

Sources of Illustrations

1 Moravske Muzeum, Brno. 2 Photo Peter Clayton. 3 BM. 4 The Metropolitan Museum of Art, New York (08.200.30). Photo Peter Clayton. 5 The Metropolitan Museum of Art, New York (31.10.8). Photo Peter Clayton. 6 Egyptian Museum, Cairo. Photo Griffith Institute, Ashmolean Museum, Oxford. 7 Archaeological Museum, Heraklion. 8 Egyptian Museum, Cairo. Photo Albert Shoucair. 9–14 BM. 15 Photo Jack Ogden. 16 The Metropolitan Museum of Art, New York, Rogers Fund, 1919 (19.2.6). All rights reserved, The Metropolitan Museum of Art. 17, 18 BM. 19 National Museum of Ireland, Dublin. 20 Photo Schweizerisches Landesmuseum, Zurich. 21 BM. 22 San Vitale, Ravenna. 23 Magyar Nemzeti Múzeum, Budapest. 24 Nationalmuseet, Copenhagen. 25 The Dumbarton Oaks Collection (Harvard University), Washington, D.C. 26 The Metropolitan Museum of Art, New York, Gift of J. Pierpont Morgan, 1917 (17.190.1664). All rights reserved, The Metropolitan Museum of Art. 27 BM. 28 The Metropolitan Museum of Art, Gift of J. Pierpont Morgan, 1917 (17.190.1670–1671). All rights reserved, The Metropolitan Museum of Art. 29 V&A. 30 Staatliche Museen zu Berlin – Preussischer Kulturbesitz – Antikensammlung. Photo Ingrid Geske. 31 Bayerisches Nationalmuseum, Munich. 32 Antikensammlung, Kunsthistorisches Museum, Vienna. 33 The Walters Art Gallery, Baltimore. 34 Museo Arqueológico Nacional, Madrid. 35, 36 BM. 37 Photo Antikvarisk-Topografiska Arkivet, Stockholm. 38 National Museum of Ireland, Dublin. 39 Trésor de la Cathédrale, Reims. 40 Staatliche Museen zu Berlin – Preussischer Kulturbesitz – Kunstgewerbemuseum. 41 Schatzkammer der Residenz, Munich. 42 V&A. 43 The Metropolitan Museum of Art, New York. Robert Lehmann Collection (1975.1.110). All rights reserved, The Metropolitan Museum of Art. 44 V&A. 45, 46 Museum zu Allerheiligen, Schaffhausen. 47 Statens Historiska Museum, Stockholm. 48 Museo del Castelvecchio, Verona. Photo Scala. 49 Carrand Collection, Museo Nazionale del Bargello, Florence. Photo Scala. 50 Schatzkammer, Kunsthistorisches Museum, Vienna. 51 The Metropolitan Museum of Art, New York, Gift of J. Pierpont Morgan, 1917 (17.190.963). All rights reserved, The Metropolitan Museum of Art. 52 Cracow Cathedral. 53 V&A. 54 Schatzkammer der Residenz, Munich. 55 V&A. 56 © Photo Bibliothèque nationale de France, Paris. 57 By courtesy of The National Portrait Gallery, London. 58 Galleria degli Uffizi, Florence. Archivi Alinari. 59 Bayerisches Nationalmuseum, Munich. 60 BM. 61 V&A. 62 BM. 63 V&A. 64 Biblioteca Ambrosiana, Milan. 65 Wernher Collection, Luton Hoo, Beds. 66 Alte Pinakothek, Munich. 67 Reproduced by permission of the Marquess of Bath, Longleat House, Warminster, Wilts. 68 Kunsthistorisches Museum, Vienna. 69 Schatzkammer der Residenz, Munich. 70 Ashmolean Museum, Oxford. 71, 72 Private collection. 73 Hatfield House. By courtesy of the Marquess of Salisbury. Photo The Fotomas Index. 74 Museum of London. 75, 76 V&A. 77 Scottish National Portrait Gallery, Edinburgh. 78, 79 V&A. 80 Museo Nacional del Prado, Madrid. 81 V&A. 82 Museum Mayer van den Bergh, Antwerp. Copyright IRPA-KIK, Brussels. 83, 84 Rijksmuseum, Amsterdam. 86, 87 V&A. 88 BM. 89 V&A. 90 Russian Diamond Fund, Moscow. Photo from Olga W. Gorewa et al., Joyaux du Trésor de Russie, La Bibliothèque des Arts, Paris, and Disertina Verlag, Disentis/Münster, 1991. 91, 92 V&A. 93 Schatzkammer der Residenz, Munich. 94 V&A. 95 © Photo Bibliothèque nationale de France, Paris. 96–100 V&A. 101 Château de Versailles. © Photo R.M.N. 102 Musée des Arts Décoratifs, Paris. Photo L. Sully-Jaulmes. 103 V&A. 104 Sotheby's, London. 105 V&A. 106 Los Angeles County Museum of Art. Gilbert Collection. 107, 108 V&A. 109 Palácio Nacional de Ajuda, Lisbon. By courtesy of P.N.A./I.P.P.A.R. 110 The Wallace Collection, London. 111 © Christie's. 112 The Russian Diamond Fund, Moscow. 113 Devonshire Collection, Chatsworth. Reproduced by permission of the Chatsworth Settlement Trustees. 114 From Ronald Sutherland Gower, Sir Thomas Lawrence, 1900. 115 V&A. 116, 117 BM. 118 Ashmolean Museum, Oxford. 119 BM. 120–123 V&A. 124 Collection: Powerhouse Museum, Sydney. Photo by Andrew Frolows. 126 Cartier Paris Archives. 127 Tiffany & Co., New York. 128 Wartski Ltd, London. 129 The Danish Museum of Decorative Art, Copenhagen. 130 Österreichisches Museum für angewandte Kunst, Vienna. 131 Musée des Arts Décoratifs, Paris. Fonds Vever. 132 Musée des Arts Décoratifs, Paris. 133 The Worshipful Company of Goldsmiths, London. 135 Private collection. 136 V&A. 137 Wartski Ltd, London. Photo Larry Stein. 138 Österreichisches Museum für angewandte Kunst, Vienna. 139, 140 V&A. 141 Charles Hosmer Morse Museum of American Art, Winter Park, Fla. 142 The Danish Museum of Decorative Art, Copenhagen. Photo Georg Jensen Museum. 143 Boucheron, Paris. 144 The Cartier Collection, Geneva. 145 Tadema Gallery, London. 146, 147 V&A. 148 The Cartier Collection, Geneva. 149 Musée des Arts Décoratifs, Paris. Fonds Fouquet. 150 ET Archives, London. 151 Sotheby's, London. 152 V&A. 153 Cartier Paris Archives. 154 Van Cleef & Arpels, Paris. 155 Sotheby's, London. 156 Courtesy Verdura, New York. 158 Courtesy Georg Jensen Museum, Copenhagen. 159 Courtesy Gijs Bakker. Photo Rien Bazen. 160 Courtesy Otto Künzli. 161 Courtesy Nel Linssen. 162 V&A. 163 Courtesy ROY. 164 The Worshipful Company of Goldsmiths, London. Courtesy Andrew Grima. 165 Private collection. Courtesy Gerda Flöckinger. Photo V&A. 166 Schmuckmuseum, Pforzheim. 167–170 V&A. 171 Courtesy Wendy Ramshaw. 172 V&A. 173 Courtesy Friedrich Becker. 174 Courtesy Bruno Martinazzi. Photo by the artist.

Index